GED
WRITING SKILLS
Part 1
Exercise Book

KARIN EVANS

Project Editor
Sarah Schmidt

CONTEMPORARY
BOOKS, INC.
CHICAGO ■ NEW YORK

Published by Contemporary Books, Inc.
180 North Michigan Avenue, Chicago, Illinois 60601
Manufactured in the United States of America
International Standard Book Number: 0-8092-4620-1

Published simultaneously in Canada by
Fitzhenry & Whiteside
91 Granton Drive
Richmond Hill, Ontario L4B 2N5
Canada

Editorial Director
Caren Van Slyke

Senior Editor
Ellen Carley Frechette

Editorial
Christine Benton
Lori Lewis-Chapman
Janice Bryant

Editorial/Production Manager
Patricia Reid

Cover Design
Lois Koehler

Art & Production
Princess Louise El
Jan Geist

Typography
Carol Schoder

CONTENTS

Introduction   1

Pre-Test   3

Sentence Basics   11

Using Verbs   21

Combining Ideas in Sentences   34

Keeping Your Story Straight   51

Capitalization and Spelling   61

Practice Test   68

Answer Key   84

INTRODUCTION

Welcome to *Contemporary's GED Writing Skills Exercise Book*. This book will help you study for the multiple-choice section of the GED Writing Skills Test for 1988–1998. The fifty worksheets in this exercise book give you additional practice in areas covered in our main GED writing textbook, *Contemporary's New GED Test 1: Writing Skills*. At the top of each worksheet, you'll see references to *text pages*. Those page numbers refer to our main GED writing textbook. Go back to the appropriate pages whenever you need a review.

This exercise book also contains a pre-test and a practice test. Before you start on the worksheets, you can take the pre-test to help you decide which writing skills to focus on. When you're finished with the worksheets, you can take the practice test. It's the same length as Part 1 of the GED Writing Skills Test, and it's in the same format.

The GED Writing Skills Test

Content Areas

The items on Part 1 of the test are taken from these content areas:

- Sentence Structure
- Usage
- Mechanics

Some questions will ask you to locate errors in sentence structure, grammar, punctuation, and spelling. Others may ask you to restate an idea in different words.

The following table presents the percentage of questions that you will be asked in each of the content areas on the GED Writing Skills Test:

Content Area	Percentage of Test
Sentence Structure	35%
Usage	35%
Mechanics	30%

Item Sets

The GED Writing Skills Test (Part 1) consists of **item sets**. Each item set begins with a paragraph that may contain errors in sentence structure, verb and pronoun usage, capitalization, spelling, and punctuation. In the questions following the paragraph, you'll be asked to correct the errors. In this exercise book, you'll find GED-type item sets in all the worksheets called "GED Practice."

Sample Item Types

There are three types of questions in these item sets—sentence correction, sentence revision, and construction shift. Here is an example of each type.

1. Sentence correction items (50 percent of the questions)

Sentence 1: **Despite it's reputation as an ugly industrial city, Pittsburgh is actually a beautiful and exciting place to live.**

What correction should be made to this sentence?

(1) replace *it's* with *its*
(2) remove the comma after *city*
(3) change *Pittsburgh* to *pittsburgh*
(4) change *is* to *be*
(5) no correction is necessary

As you can see, several different types of errors are suggested in the answer choices. You have to decide whether there is a spelling error, a punctuation error, a capitalization error, a verb form error, or no error at all. Sometimes the fifth option, *no correction is necessary*, will be the correct answer. Not all items, however, will have that option. The correct answer for this item is choice (1).

2. Sentence revision items (35 percent of the questions)

Sentence 2: **In Goldsboro, North Carolina, preservationists is restoring some gracious old mansions**.

Which of the following is the best way to write the underlined portion of this sentence? If you think the original is the best way to write the sentence, choose option (1).

(1) is
(2) would
(3) was
(4) are
(5) will have

With this type of item, you have to focus on only one part of the sentence—the underlined part. The first answer choice is always the same as the original sentence. Only one type of error is tested in this sample item: subject–verb agreement. In this item, the correct answer is choice (4).

You'll begin practicing these sentence correction and sentence revision items early in this workbook, starting with Worksheet 9.

3. Construction shift items (15 percent of the questions)

In these items, the sentences are *not* incorrect. Instead of asking you to correct errors, these items ask you to combine or rewrite sentences.

Sentence 3: **People in fantastic costumes mob the downtown streets of Boulder, Colorado, on Halloween night**.

If you rewrote this sentence beginning with

On Halloween night the downtown streets of Boulder, Colorado,

the next word should be

(1) people
(2) mob
(3) when
(4) costumes
(5) are

To answer this item, you need to rewrite the sentence in your head. Your goal is to preserve the meaning of the original sentence. If you don't see the correct answer right away, try each answer choice in turn to see which one makes sense. The correct answer is choice (5): *On Halloween night the downtown streets of Boulder, Colorado, are mobbed with people in fantastic costumes.*

You won't see any construction shift items in your GED Practice worksheets until Worksheet 32. By then you should be ready to tackle this type of item.

For more information about all three item types and how to answer them, turn to Chapter 7 in Contemporary's main GED writing textbook, *New GED Test 1: Writing Skills*.

PRE-TEST

This pre-test will help you identify worksheets in this book that you should focus on. The pre-test is in five sections. Read the directions carefully for each section. Do the best you can and don't worry if you have trouble. It's fine to leave questions blank.

Section 1

Directions: Each of the following sentences contains one error. Rewrite each sentence to correct it. Some of the sentences may be fragments—incomplete thoughts. Add an idea of your own to make a complete sentence.

Example: Mike gave she a yellow sweater for her birthday.

Mike gave her a yellow sweater for her birthday.

1. We bought a loaf of bread, a stick of butter, and a bottle of orange juice, for breakfast.

   _____

2. Plans for the holidays.

   _____

3. I gave back there Sunday paper.

   _____

4. Lisa let her employee's take the day off.

   _____

5. Bring your childrens old clothing to the school on Saturday.

   _____

6. Him takes the bus to work with Jeanette.

   _____

7. To spend more time with my family.

   _____

8. Lester and me are headed to the lake for a swim.

   _____

9. Greg and Mindy forgot to take they lunch.

   _____

10. Your not telling the truth.

    _____

11. Swimming walking, and biking are good types of exercise for your heart.

_____

12. During the game, all of the athletes wallets were stolen.

_____

Section 2

Directions: Choose the verb that completes each sentence correctly. Pay close attention to subject-verb agreement and clues to verb tense.

1. Either Martha or Clara (*take, takes*) care of their grandmother every weekend.

2. The world leaders (*discussed, will discuss, discuss*) the treaty last night.

3. The passengers (*were riding, were rideing*) the subway toward Bleeker Street.

4. In Glen Morgan Park (*is, are, be*) statues of Civil War heroes.

5. Good jobs (*been, have been, will be*) hard to find lately in Hewsonville.

6. All of the water in the county (*was, were*) tested.

7. Why (*don't, doesn't*) they vote?

8. Neither the two boys nor their mother (*know, knows*) about the surprise.

9. Rodney Raider (*is sing, sung, sang*) classic rock tunes of the 1950s.

10. By Christmas, the men in the class (*will have knitted, has knitted*) sweaters for their wives.

11. Ms. Jasculca (*is writting, is writing*) her paper on *The Color Purple*.

12. Everyone (*go, goes*) into The Twilight Room for cocktails and dancing.

13. The workers on break (*mix, mixes, mixs*) instant coffee and hot cocoa for a quick drink.

14. Every year the list of children's names (*growes, grows, grow*) a little longer.

15. Next week Caroline (*will run, runs, ran*) for secretary of the student association.

Section 3

Directions: Each of the following sentences has an underlined section that may contain an error. Choose the option that makes the underlined section correct. If there is no error in the sentence, choose option (1).

1. Students in adult education programs come from widely varying <u>backgrounds and they</u> have very different needs.

   (1) backgrounds and they
   (2) backgrounds; and they
   (3) backgrounds, and they

2. The daily newspaper is <u>inexpensive; therefore, it</u> contains interesting articles for almost anybody.

   (1) inexpensive; therefore, it
   (2) inexpensive, therefore it
   (3) inexpensive; furthermore, it

3. You need to know fractions to increase and decrease <u>recipes, you</u> might need one-half of three-fourths of a cup of flour.

   (1) recipes, you
   (2) recipes; for example, you
   (3) recipes, but you

4. Calculators make math <u>easier, but we</u> still need to know whether to add, subtract, multiply, or divide.

   (1) easier, but we
   (2) easier, and we
   (3) easier but still

5. When you park at a broken parking <u>meter, put</u> a note for the police under your wiper.

   (1) meter, put
   (2) meter put
   (3) meter; then put

6. Writing a letter takes <u>time it</u> can really brighten another person's day.

   (1) time it
   (2) time, yet it
   (3) time, for it

7. After Katie Peabody had her first <u>child, she divorces</u> her husband.

   (1) child, she divorces
   (2) child, she divorced
   (3) child; then she divorced

8. Jenny Rabin was wearing <u>jeans, consequently,</u> she was not allowed into the nightclub.

    (1) jeans, consequently,
    (2) jeans; consequently,
    (3) jeans; for example,

9. Because Greg <u>felt</u> lonely living by himself in an apartment, he adopted a kitten.

    (1) felt
    (2) will feel
    (3) will be feeling

10. Secretaries never have to type the same thing <u>twice if they</u> use word processors.

    (1) twice if they
    (2) twice unless they
    (3) twice before they

Section 4

Directions: Each of the following sentences has an underlined section that may contain an error. Choose the option that makes the underlined section correct. If there is no error in the sentence, choose option (1).

1. <u>Sipping coffee nervously, Ms. Bates'</u> test results came back from the lab.

    (1) Sipping coffee nervously, Ms. Bates'
    (2) While Ms. Bates was sipping coffee nervously, her
    (3) While sipping coffee nervously Ms. Bates

2. An old brass lamp from a garage sale can look great after <u>they are</u> polished up.

    (1) they are
    (2) you are
    (3) it is

3. The city could make the neighborhood much safer if <u>they</u> put up more streetlights.

    (1) they
    (2) it
    (3) their

4. Alfred arrived at the Halloween party wearing plaid boxer shorts, <u>high-top sneakers</u>, and a Hawaiian tie.

    (1) high-top sneakers
    (2) with high-top sneakers
    (3) wearing high-top sneakers

5. <u>KinderSchool a chain of day-care centers</u> has a reputation for creative programs for very young children.

   (1) KinderSchool a chain of day-care centers has
   (2) KinderSchool, a chain of day-care centers has
   (3) KinderSchool, a chain of day-care centers, has

6. A group of talented young <u>musicians played classical music, ages eleven through fifteen, after the PTA spaghetti dinner.</u>

   (1) musicians played classical music, ages eleven through fifteen, after the PTA spaghetti dinner.
   (2) musicians played classical music after the PTA spaghetti dinner, ages eleven through fifteen.
   (3) musicians, ages eleven through fifteen, played classical music after the PTA spaghetti dinner.

7. Chiropractic doctors heal people by adjusting vertebrae in their necks and backs, giving them nutrition supplements, and <u>with other natural methods.</u>

   (1) with other natural methods
   (2) using other natural methods
   (3) other natural methods

8. Neither Sylvia nor Katherine has finished writing <u>her</u> essay yet.

   (1) her
   (2) their
   (3) one's

9. Your paycheck cannot be signed by the office <u>without receiving</u> your completed time card.

   (1) without receiving
   (2) unless it receives
   (3) unless they receive

10. Mrs. Adams and Mrs. Gallivan took <u>her</u> daughter to lunch at the Walnut Room after the graduation ceremony.

    (1) her
    (2) their
    (3) Mrs. Gallivan's

Section 5

Directions: Each of the following sentences contains one error in spelling or capitalization. Cross out the error and write in the correction.

1. The site of the new Building for Roane State Community College is on Alexander Drive.

2. We are certein that the city council will approve funding for the project.

3. Though it's a long distance to drive, the Fall colors are breathtaking on the Blue Ridge Parkway.

4. Today in Carson city, Nevada, the governor congratulated the new senators.

5. Upon her death, the valuable chrystal glasses were given to the Art Institute of Chicago.

6. Many married couples struggling to concieve visit doctors who specialize in fertility problems.

7. It's all right with me if alot of your relatives come to our anniversary dinner.

8. The affect of the conversation between Matthew and his counselor is unknown at this time.

9. Rana usually takes the old country road that lies East of the main highway.

10. Takana's sister-in-law, who is also japanese, writes a column for several foreign-language newspapers in the United States.

Answers start on page 9.

Pre-Test Answer Key

SECTION 1

1. We bought a loaf of bread, a stick of butter, and a bottle of orange **juice for** breakfast.
2. **We have made our** plans for the holidays. (The original sentence was a fragment. Any complete sentence is a correct answer.)
3. I gave back **their** Sunday paper.
4. Lisa let her **employees** take the day off.
5. Bring your **children's** old clothing to the school on Saturday.
6. **He** takes the bus to work with Jeanette.
7. **I need to** spend more time with my family. (The original sentence was a fragment. Any complete sentence is a correct answer.)
8. Lester and **I** are headed to the lake for a swim.
9. Greg and Mindy forgot to take **their** lunch.
10. **You're** not telling the truth.
11. **Swimming, walking**, and biking are good types of exercise for your heart.
12. During the game, all of the **athletes'** wallets were stolen.

SECTION 2

1. takes
2. discussed
3. were riding
4. are
5. have been
6. was
7. don't
8. knows
9. sang
10. will have knitted
11. is writing
12. goes
13. mix
14. grows
15. will run

SECTION 3

1. (3)
2. (3)
3. (2)
4. (1)
5. (1)
6. (2)
7. (2)
8. (2)
9. (1)
10. (1)

SECTION 4

1. (2)
2. (3)
3. (2)
4. (1)
5. (3)
6. (3)
7. (2)
8. (1)
9. (2)
10. (3)

SECTION 5

1. building
2. certain
3. fall
4. City
5. crystal
6. conceive
7. a lot
8. effect
9. east
10. Japanese

Pre-Test Evaluation Chart

Use the chart below to determine the writing skills areas in which you need to do the most work. Circle any items that you got wrong and pay particular attention to areas where you missed half or more of the questions. The column called "Satellite Review Pages" lists pages in Contemporary's *New GED Writing Skills Test,* and the column called "Exercise Book Review Pages" lists pages in this book. Refer to the appropriate pages when you need practice or review.

Skill Area	Item Number	Satellite Review Pages	Exercise Book Review Pages	Total Correct
Section One				
Basic Sentence Structure	1, 2, 7, 11	30–43	11–13	_____/4
Nouns and Pronouns	3, 4, 5, 6, 8, 9, 10, 12	44–57	14–17	_____/8
Section Two				
Verb Form and Tense	2, 3, 5, 9, 10, 11, 13, 14, 15	71–91	21–27	_____/9
Subject–Verb Agreement	1, 4, 6, 7, 8, 12	92–105	28–30	_____/6
Section Three				
Compound Sentences	1, 2, 3, 4, 6, 8	128–39	34–37	_____/6
Complex Sentences	5, 7, 9, 10	139–48	38–46	_____/4
Section Four				
Sentence Structure Problems	1, 4, 5, 6, 7, 9	182–94	51–56	_____/6
Pronoun Agreement	2, 3, 8, 10	195–205	57	_____/4
Section Five				
Capitalization	1, 3, 4, 9, 10	237–41	61	_____/5
Spelling	2, 5, 6, 7, 8	241–58	62–64	_____/5

Total Correct _____/57

SENTENCE BASICS

Worksheet 1
Identifying and Rewriting Fragments

A *complete sentence* must pass three tests: (1) It must have a subject that tells whom or what the sentence is about. (2) It must have a predicate that tells what the subject is or does. (3) It must express a complete thought.

A group of words that does *not* pass these three tests is called a *fragment*.

Text pages 30-35

FRAGMENT: Got grease on his clothes.
COMPLETE SENTENCE: Sam got grease on his clothes.

Part A

Directions: Mark each of the following groups of words with an *F* if it is a fragment or with an *S* if it is a complete sentence. Then, on a separate sheet of paper, rewrite each fragment as a complete sentence.

___*F*___ **1.** In many states, pedestrian crosswalks.

_____ **2.** Come to a complete stop at stop signs.

_____ **3.** Worn tires make skids more likely.

_____ **4.** At the top of a freeway entrance ramp.

_____ **5.** Do tailgaters tempt you to slam on your brakes?

_____ **6.** Safe drivers reduce their speed in the rain.

_____ **7.** Result in higher insurance rates.

_____ **8.** When changing lanes.

_____ **9.** A learner's permit allows.

_____ **10.** Wearing a seatbelt could save your life.

Part B

Directions: Underline the fragments in the following paragraph. Then, on a separate sheet of paper, rewrite the paragraph, eliminating all the fragments. You may add words or combine fragments if necessary.

More and more people are volunteering their time. To help others. As many as 40 percent of adults report doing charitable work. Involved in helping the elderly. They might visit nursing homes, for example. Programs for youth like Big Brothers and Big Sisters. Volunteers also work in Boys' Clubs, Girls' Clubs, and other community programs for children. Churches often encourage people to volunteer. By telling their members where their help is needed.

Answers start on page 84.

11

Worksheet 2
Identifying the Simple Subject and Verb

Text pages
35-41

The skeleton of a sentence is the simple subject and the verb. The **simple subject** is the key word in the sentence that tells whom or what the sentence is about. The **verb** is the part of the predicate that tells what that subject is or does.

When you look for the simple subject and verb in a sentence, keep in mind that sometimes the verb (or part of the verb) comes before the subject.

There is only one more present for you to open.
VERB   SUBJECT

In one type of sentence, the subject is not written, but it is understood to be *you*. This kind of sentence, called a **command**, gives a direction or an order.

Bring me some milk and cookies. (*The understood subject is* you.)

Directions: Complete the following exercise, filling in the simple subject and the verb for each sentence. Remember that sometimes a verb consists of more than one word.

	Simple Subject	Verb
1. The pope asked for an end to the arms race.	*pope*	*asked*
2. Measure your ingredients carefully for the best results.		
3. There are seven candidates in the mayoral primary.		
4. Should values be part of our children's school curriculum?		
5. Farmers sell fresh produce at the farmer's market on Lee Street every Saturday.		
6. On exhibit at the Wilson Arts Center are paintings by Linda Greyson.		
7. Tell your two-timing husband good-bye.		
8. Members of the council voted unanimously for the zoning ordinance.		
9. Why do fools fall in love?		
10. Here are records of the settlers of Chatham County in the 1750s.		
11. At the forum were many supporters of the proposed ban on nonreturnable bottles.		
12. Box office receipts totaled $12 million.		
13. Take home two dresses for the price of one!		
14. Have you checked your blood pressure lately?		
15. There lived the inventor of the flyswatter.		

Answers start on page 84.

Worksheet 3
Practice with Compounding

Compounding is connecting two or more equally important sentence parts with a conjunction (*and, or,* or *but*). When three or more compound elements are connected in a series, they must be separated with commas.

Text pages 41-43

For example, the following three sentences all have the same subject. They can be combined using a compound predicate. Note the use of commas.

> The audience laughed. The audience cried. The audience
>   cheered.   (*and*)
> The audience laughed, cried, **and** cheered.

Directions: Combine the following sets of sentences by compounding. Use the conjunction given and make any other necessary changes in wording. Clues are given when a verb change is necessary. Be sure to punctuate correctly.

1. Principals need leadership skills. Superintendents need leadership skills. Administrators need leadership skills. (*and*)

2. Homeless people sleep in the building at night. The homeless people must leave by 6:00 A.M. (*but*)

3. Sirens disturb the neighborhood. Barking dogs disturb the neighborhood. (*and*)

4. The cause of the food poisoning could have been the meat. The cause of the food poisoning could have been the potato salad. The cause of the food poisoning could have been the milk. (*or*)

5. Brisk walking is good aerobic exercise. Swimming is good aerobic exercise. Cycling is good aerobic exercise. (*and; is ⟶ are*).

6. A recent poll showed that Americans are buying less beef. A recent poll showed that Americans are buying more chicken. (*and*)

7. This state allows girls to marry at the age of fifteen. This state prevents boys from marrying before the age of seventeen. (*but*)

8. Payton caught the forty-yard pass. Payton ran the ball twenty-five yards. Payton scored a spectacular touchdown. (*and*)

9. Wealthy parents can choose private schools for their children. Wealthy parents can choose public schools for their children. (*or*)

10. Tasteless humor makes this film poor entertainment. Mechanical acting makes this film poor entertainment. (*and; makes ⟶ make*)

Answers start on page 84.

Worksheet 4
Using Possessive and Plural Nouns

Text pages
45-50

The *plurals* of nouns are used to show more than one person, place, or thing. Most plurals are formed by adding the letter *s* to a word (*sentence*——▶*sentences*). If a consonant precedes a *y*, be sure to change the *y* to *i* and add *es* (*baby*——▶*babies*). In a few cases, the form of the word changes in the plural form (*child*——▶*children*).

The possessive of singular nouns is formed by adding *'s* (*brother*——▶ *brother's sweater*). The possessive of plural nouns ending in *s* is formed by adding just an apostrophe (*brothers*——▶*brothers' sweater*). However, if a plural does not end in *s*, the possessive ending is *'s* (*children's toys*).

Directions: Check the following sentences carefully for errors in plural and possessive forms of nouns. Each sentence contains one error. Circle the incorrect noun in each sentence and write the correct form in the blank.

Example: The community center provides valuable (service's) to senior citizens.   *services*
                                        _____

1. The reform of divorce laws in the 1970s was supposed to   _____
   help womans trapped in bad marriages.

2. The new divorce lawes have actually trapped many   _____
   women in poverty.

3. An ex-husband is often able to walk away from a divorce   _____
   with most of his families' income and assets.

4. Typically, ex-husbands have more work experience and   _____
   earn more money than ex-wifes.

5. In addition, many mens who are ordered to pay child   _____
   support or alimony don't make these payments.

6. As a result, their former wife's and children can fall on   _____
   hard times after the divorce.

7. Many lawmakers now believe that penaltys for men (and   _____
   women) who abandon their families should be stiffer.

8. Some states are making it tougher for parents to avoid   _____
   paying for their childrens' support.

9. For example, Wisconsin now takes child support payments   _____
   directly from a parents paycheck.

10. And in New York, judge's must follow new guidelines that   _____
    consider the earning power of both spouses in setting
    alimony.

11. Other state's rules are changing as well, as legislatures in   _____
    California, Texas, and Massachusetts follow Wisconsin's or
    New York's lead.

12. Increases in single mother's incomes will especially benefit   _____
    children of divorced parents.

Answers start on page 84.

Worksheet 5
Identifying Antecedents

A *pronoun* is a word that replaces and refers to a noun. The noun that a pronoun refers to is called its *antecedent*. The antecedent of a pronoun may be in the same sentence, or it may be nearby in another sentence.

Text pages 50-51

Many **people** put **their** money in savings accounts. **They** try to save for vacations or unexpected expenses.

Directions: Each pronoun in the following paragraph has a number underneath it. Write the antecedent of each pronoun in the numbered blanks below the paragraph.

In the early 1960s, many Americans built bomb shelters in their
                                                              1

basements and backyards. They built the shelters because they
                        2   3

feared a nuclear war. The shelters are still there today, but they are
                                                             4

being put to peacetime use. One woman's shelter was taken over by

her nephew—he used it as a playroom. Another couple chuckles at
5   6   7

the boxy pink structure in their backyard. They would like to use it
                            8   9   10

as a playhouse, but it has no windows. However, some shelter
                     11

owners think they are better off preserving the shelters for their
                 12   13

original use. One man says he would rather have a shelter and not
                           14

need it than not have it at all.
     15   16

1. _Americans_   9. _____

2. _____   10. _____

3. _____   11. _____

4. _____   12. _____

5. _____   13. _____

6. _____   14. _____

7. _____   15. _____

8. _____   16. _____

Answers start on page 84.

Worksheet 6
Choosing Subject, Object, and Possessive Pronouns

Text pages
51-53

Basic Pronoun Forms			
Subject	**Object**	**Possessive**	
I	me	my	mine
you	you	your	yours
he	him	his	his
she	her	her	hers
it	it	its	its
we	us	our	ours
they	them	their	theirs

Directions: Each of the following sentences contains a blank. Fill in the blank with a subject, an object, or a possessive pronoun from the chart above. There are several possible correct answers for all of the blanks.

1. Give _____*him*_____ a chance.

2. _____ testified before the grand jury yesterday.

3. _____ research found that tropical oils such as palm and coconut oil have bad health effects.

4. Why had _____ not been told of the danger?

5. The mayor presented _____ with the key to the city.

6. Will _____ be willing to sign the petition?

7. In June of last year, _____ home was destroyed by fire.

8. _____ will visit twelve cities on this campaign tour.

9. These unsigned works of art are thought to be _____ .

10. The new program will allow _____ to learn new job skills.

11. Knowledge of edible plants helped _____ survive in the wilderness.

12. A judge ruled that the disputed land is _____ .

13. _____ wrote a letter of complaint to the company in June.

14. _____ children are doing well in school.

15. The tenants filed a complaint against _____ .

Answers start on page 85.

Worksheet 7
Problems with Pronouns

Directions: Underline the correct choice to complete each of the following sentences.

Text pages
54-57

1. The supervisor and (*I, me*) filled out the grievance form.

2. (*Its, It's*) no way to make a living.

3. James and (*she, her*) can repair the equipment at any time.

4. (*Their, They're*) working hard to complete the project on schedule.

5. (*Your, You're*) bookkeeping skills will give you an edge in the job market.

6. Give the data you have collected to Dr. Reisner and (*they, them*).

7. (*Whose, Who's*) going to get the promotion?

8. Leadership ability makes (*she, her*) and Lauren valuable members of the association.

9. I can't locate (*its, it's*) power switch.

10. (*She, Her*) and Horace counted forty-seven copy machine breakdowns last month.

11. (*Its, It's*) instruction manual is written in Japanese.

12. (*Theirs, There's*) is the one on the right.

13. The manager asked to see Martin and (*we, us*) in his office.

14. My guess is that (*theirs, there's*) nothing wrong with it.

15. (*Whose, Who's*) turn is it to make the coffee?

16. (*They, Them*) and (*we, us*) have developed a plan to streamline production.

17. The company's policies allowed Marcia and (*I, me*) to take maternity leave.

18. (*Your, You're*) not serious, are you?

19. Every summer, (*they, them*) and their spouses are invited to spend a day swimming and picnicking.

20. Let me know if (*your, you're*) going to be out of the office.

Answers start on page 85.

Worksheet 8
Sentence Basics Editing Review

Text pages
30-57

Directions: Rewrite the following paragraph on a separate sheet of paper, correcting all the errors. You'll need to check for all the types of errors you've practiced correcting in Worksheets 1-7. Revise this paragraph for correct use of

☑ complete sentences

☑ compound elements

☑ possessives and plurals

☑ pronoun forms

Programs for mildly retarded teenagers. Teach them basic life skills for more independent living. In one program, retarded teenagers come to school at a model apartment. At this school for living, the teen's learn how to cook, and clean. Their taught skills as simple as how to hold a broom and sweep. More complicated skills like cooking breakfasts lunchs, and dinners. Them and they're teachers also take trips outside the apartment. The students learn to order in restaurantes, ride buses, and pay for movies and bowling. Parents report that the students's new skills are a big help at home. One mother says that she's daughter now makes all the beds with hospital corners!

Answers start on page 85.

Worksheet 9
GED Practice in Sentence Basics

Directions: Read the following passage completely, looking for errors like the ones you have practiced correcting in Worksheets 1-8. Then answer the questions about individual sentences in the passage.

Text pages 30-62

(1) Products containing ingredients derived from seaweed about fifteen times a day. (2) Seaweed extracts are used in toothpastes shaving creams, diet salad dressings, and beer. (3) The Japanese consume such large amounts of this nutritious vegetable that their unable to produce enough of it.

(4) Although there's a big market for seaweed, U.S. companys have not been producing it. (5) However, recent discoveries may make seaweed farming profitable along certain stretchs of North Carolina's coast. (6) Have developed an artificial method of rearing the plants called *cell culturing.* (7) Cell culturing speeds up the seaweeds normal rate of reproduction. (8) The type's of seaweed that grow naturally in North Carolina respond well to cell culturing. (9) Scientists working on the project hope to keep their experimental seaweed beds' producing twelve months a year. (10) The researchers say that eventually seaweed will be a profitable, simple crop to raise.

1. Sentence 1: **Products containing ingredients derived from seaweed about fifteen times a day.**

Which of the following is the best way to write the underlined portion of this sentence? If you think the original is the best way, choose option (1).

   (1) Products
   (2) Using products
   (3) We use products
   (4) Products'
   (5) Product's

2. Sentence 2: **Seaweed extracts are used in toothpastes shaving creams, diet salad dressings, and beer.**

What correction should be made to this sentence?

   (1) change *extracts* to *extract's*
   (2) insert a comma after *toothpastes*
   (3) change the spelling of *creams* to *creames*
   (4) remove the comma after *dressings*
   (5) no correction is necessary

3. Sentence 3: **The Japanese consume such large amounts of this nutritious vegetable that their unable to produce enough of it.**

Which of the following is the best way to write the underlined portion of this sentence? If you think the original is the best way to write the sentence, choose option (1).

   (1) their
   (2) they
   (3) them
   (4) they're
   (5) there

4. Sentence 4: **Although there's a big market for seaweed, U.S. companys have not been producing it.**

What correction should be made to this sentence?

   (1) replace *there's* with *theirs*
   (2) change the spelling of *companys* to *companies*
   (3) change *companys* to *company's*
   (4) replace *it* with *them*
   (5) no correction is necessary

5. Sentence 5: **However, recent discoveries may make seaweed farming profitable along certain stretchs of North Carolina's coast.**

   Which of the following is the best way to write the underlined portion of this sentence? If you think the original is the best way, choose option (1).

   (1) stretchs
   (2) stretches
   (3) stretches'
   (4) stretch's
   (5) stretchs'

6. Sentence 6: **Have developed an artificial method of rearing the plants called *cell culturing*.**

   Which of the following is the best way to write the underlined portion of this sentence? If you think the original is the best way, choose option (1).

   (1) Have developed
   (2) Developed
   (3) Have been developing
   (4) Scientists
   (5) Scientists have developed

7. Sentence 7: **Cell culturing speeds up the seaweeds normal rate of reproduction.**

   Which of the following is the best way to write the underlined portion of this sentence? If you think the original is the best way, choose option (1).

   (1) seaweeds
   (2) seaweed'
   (3) seaweeds's
   (4) seaweed's
   (5) seaweedes

8. Sentence 8: **The type's of seaweed that grow naturally in North Carolina respond well to cell culturing.**

   Which of the following is the best way to write the underlined portion of this sentence? If you think the original is the best way, choose option (1).

   (1) type's
   (2) types'
   (3) types's
   (4) type'
   (5) types

9. Sentence 9: **Scientists working on the project hope to keep their experimental seaweed beds' producing twelve months a year.**

   What correction should be made to this sentence?

   (1) change *Scientists* to *Scientists'*
   (2) replace *their* with *they're*
   (3) change *beds'* to *beds*
   (4) change the spelling of *months* to *monthes*
   (5) no correction is necessary

   Answers start on page 85.

USING VERBS

Worksheet 10
Simple and Continuing Tenses

Verb tenses are used to show the time that something happens. The examples below illustrate the simple present, past, and future and the continuing tenses. The continuing tenses, shown in the second sentence of each example, are used to show action that is ongoing in the present, past, or future.

Text pages 71-75

> PRESENT: Jack **walks** to work every day. Jack **is walking** to work this morning.
> PAST: Rachel **drove** her car. Rachel **was driving** her car at the time.
> FUTURE: Matt **will take** the bus. Matt **will be taking** the bus daily.

Directions: Complete each sentence by writing the correct form of the verb in the blank. You'll need to use the simple and continuing tenses. Check each sentence carefully for time clues to the correct tense. More than one answer may be correct in some sentences.

1. (*read*) In this journalism class, students _____*read*_____ the newspaper every day.

2. (*run*) Currently a black candidate _____ for alderman in that ward.

3. (*elect*) Yesterday English voters _____ the prime minister to another term in office.

4. (*appear*) Rock star Little Larry _____ at the Blue Mountain Festival this coming Sunday.

5. (*consider*) A senate committee currently _____ a national health insurance plan.

6. (*load*) Ms. Butzin _____ crates on the truck at the time of the accident.

7. (*pour*) It _____ rain by late this afternoon, according to the National Weather Service.

8. (*complete*) Next year Marti _____ her degree in physical therapy.

9. (*pay*) At present, the city _____ private contractors to repair the roads.

10. (*watch*) At 8:00 tonight, the children _____ their mother graduate from college.

Answers start on page 85.

21

Worksheet 11
Using the Perfect Tenses

Text pages
76-78

The *perfect tenses* are used to show action completed before a specific time in the past or continuing to a specific time in the future.

PRESENT PERFECT: The workers **have complained** about the broken heater.
PAST PERFECT: By last Friday, they **had worked** without heat for two weeks.
FUTURE PERFECT: By next Monday, they **will have decided** whether to go on strike.

Directions: Complete each sentence by writing the correct form of the verb in the blank. You'll need to use the present perfect, past perfect, and future perfect tenses. Check each sentence carefully for time clues to the correct tense.

1. (*form*) Over time, the sand dunes *have formed* a natural barrier between the highway and the ocean.

2. (*wash*) By the end of next year, the waves _____ the beach away completely.

3. (*learn*) The bikers _____ first aid before starting out last year.

4. (*entertain*) Three months from now, the dancers _____ 25,000 people in eighteen cities.

5. (*claim*) By 1920, many branches of the Ashton family _____ homesteads in this area.

6. (*guard*) Jeremiah McDonald _____ this part of the museum since 1965.

7. (*board*) Two hours from now, all 231 members of the ship's crew _____ .

8. (*market*) The Si-Kon Company _____ farm products in the Midwest before its collapse in 1985.

9. (*reflect*) Since last year, your utility bills _____ cost overruns at the nuclear power plant.

10. (*construct*) Recently the Parks and Recreation Department _____ several recycling bins.

11. (*travel*) By the end of this year, Fulton _____ 25,000 miles in his search for the perfect hamburger.

12. (*accept*) By the end of yesterday's meeting, Ms. Jaffee _____ the position.

13. (*thrill*) Before its first half hour was over, last night's drama _____ viewers of all ages.

14. (*borrow*) They _____ my vacuum cleaner every week for two years.

15. (*select*) Joan Redding _____ the books for the course by tomorrow.

Answers start on page 85.

Worksheet 12
Review of Regular Verb Tenses

Directions: The verb in each of the following sentences has been left out. Choose the correct verb to complete each sentence. Be sure to pay attention to time clues and look for correct spellings.

Text pages 71-83

1. Rock Hudson _____ of AIDS in the mid-1980s.

    a. dyed   **b.** dying   **c.** died

2. In a popular old movie, Katharine Hepburn _____ Spencer Tracy.

    a. marries   **b.** will marry   **c.** marrys

3. Paul Newman's popularity never _____ over the past 40 years.

    a. will waver   **b.** has wavered   **c.** wavers

4. A traditional Amish community _____ in the suspenseful film *Witness.*

    a. portrayed   **b.** was portrayed   **c.** was portraying

5. *Singing in the Rain* _____ to delight today's audiences.

    a. continues   **b.** was continuing   **c.** had continued

6. Before seeing Jimmy Stewart's first movie, my grandmother _____ Clark Gable.

    a. was preferring   **b.** had prefered   **c.** had preferred

7. After tomorrow night's show, I _____ *It's a Wonderful Life* eight times.

    a. will have watched   **b.** watched   **c.** have watched

8. Since its debut in 1977, millions _____ in wonder at the special effects in the movie *Star Wars.*

    a. gazed   **b.** have gazed   **c.** are gazing

Answers start on page 85.

Worksheet 13
Unfinished Sentences

Text pages
71-83

Directions: Using the verb indicated, complete the following sentences. Use your imagination! Make sure that you choose a verb tense according to the time clue in the sentence.

1. (*walk*) Last night, Martha *walked three miles to see her boyfriend.*

   _____

2. (*give*) Tomorrow I _____

   _____

3. (*complete*) By midnight tonight, _____

   _____

4. (*jump*) Since last June, Herman _____

   _____

5. (*control*) In the future, computers _____

   _____

6. (*hurry*) At the moment, Ms. Peabody _____

   _____

7. (*drive*) Every day _____

   _____

8. (*live*) Ten years ago, my family _____

   _____

9. (*hop*) All next week, _____

   _____

10. (*laugh*) In general, _____

    _____

11. (*open*) By noon yesterday, Lester _____

    _____

12. (*roll*) For ten years now, Aunt Bertha _____

    _____

Answers will vary.

Worksheet 14
Writing Irregular Verbs

Directions: Write the correct form of the irregular verb to complete each sentence. Remember that the past participle needs a helping verb (*has, have,* or *had*). If there is a helping verb, use the past participle and underline the helping verb. If there is no helping verb, use the simple past.

Text pages 83-87

1. (*write*) a. The students _____ *wrote* _____ a 200-word essay on yesterday's exam.

   b. The students <u>have</u> _____ *written* _____ essays before.

2. (*take*) a. The paramedics have _____ the victim to the hospital.

   b. Horace Williams _____ twelve years to write his novel.

3. (*begin*) a. I have not yet _____ to fight.

   b. Johanna Ault _____ to lose her hair after several radiation treatments.

4. (*see*) a. The governor has _____ the proposed legislation.

   b. Mrs. McGillicuddy _____ her daughter fall into the water.

5. (*drink*) a. The children _____ Kool-aid and ate fruit and sandwiches.

   b. The driver had _____ two quarts of beer by the time he was stopped by the police.

6. (*freeze*) a. My grandmother nearly _____ one winter as a child in South Dakota.

   b. The wet clothes on the line have _____ .

7. (*ride*) a. Cowboys _____ through this pass many years ago, right where those condos are.

   b. Chester has never _____ on a tractor before.

8. (*wear*) a. Mom _____ her thermal underwear to bed last night because of the cold.

   b. Michael had _____ a tuxedo only once before his wedding day.

Answers start on page 86.

Worksheet 15
More Irregular Verbs

Text pages
87-89

Directions: Write the correct form of the irregular verb to complete each sentence. Remember that the past participle needs a helping verb. If there is a helping verb, use the past participle and underline the helping verb. If there is no helping verb, use the simple past.

1. (*bit*) Dogs roaming around the complex <u>have</u> _____*bitten*_____ several children.

2. (*fly*) Shultz _____ to Beirut yesterday to meet with Middle Eastern leaders.

3. (*teach*) Last year a volunteer in the Randolph County literacy program _____ Benson to read.

4. (*buy*) Fans of the popular television star Miller Mayfield have _____ thousands of copies of his book.

5. (*swear*) The colonel's secretary _____ under oath that the documents were intact.

6. (*pay*) Have you _____ for one too many repairs on your old car?

7. (*stand*) Over the years, Amnesty International has _____ for human rights around the world.

8. (*understand*) She has never _____ why her family stayed in New York City.

9. (*sleep*) The guard _____ through the alarm, allowing the thieves to escape unnoticed.

10. (*hold*) Earlier today, the parents _____ their premature baby for the first time.

11. (*hear*) Has Mr. Martin _____ of the wonders of this new product?

12. (*find*) Researchers have _____ that many violent criminals have brain damage.

13. (*mean*) Before his death, Falana _____ to tell his family where he buried his fortune.

14. (*cost*) Last summer a pool pass _____ $37 per family.

Answers start on page 86.

Worksheet 16
Verb Tense in a Passage

Directions: Each of the following passages contains three errors in verb tense. Underline all the verbs in each passage; then correct the verbs that are wrong.

Text page 91

Passage 1

William Rathje, a professor at the University of Arizona, studies "garbology." He and his students sort and study samples of garbage from all types of neighborhoods. Their findings are quite interesting. For example, middle-income families waste more food than upper- or lower-income families. They also bought more name brands. The average household discards more than 13,000 paper items each year and tossed out more than 1,800 plastic items. Rathje is especially concerned about plastic garbage. Plastics are hard to recycle, use up valuable petroleum, and gave off toxic chemicals when burned.

Passage 2

In the mid-1980s, the country music industry was in crisis. The big stars were seeing their record sales plummet. Nashville, the country music capital of the world, panicks. But now country music is making a big comeback with new sounds and new artists. The sentimental pop-style arrangements of the early 1980s are disappearing. Today artists will be looking back to Texas swing, 1950s honky-tonk and rockabilly, and bluegrass for inspiration. Record companies are competing madly for these artists. Their record sales were climbing. The Nashville guard is changing.

Answers start on page 86.

Worksheet 17
Basic Subject-Verb Agreement

Text pages
92-95

Basic Rules for Subject-Verb Agreement:

1. The present-tense verbs of singular subjects (except *I* and *you*) end in *s* or *es*:

> I **run** two miles every day.
> He **runs** two miles every day.

2. The present-tense verbs of plural subjects do not end in *s*:

> We **run** two miles together every day.

Directions: Identify the subject of each sentence. Then underline the form of the verb that agrees with the subject.

1. We all (*pick, picks*) our own poison when it comes to food.

2. Fresh garlic (*are, is*) an aromatic, flavorful seasoning.

3. Brown rice (*contain, contains*) more vitamins and fiber than white rice.

4. Potato salad (*make, makes*) a great hot-weather main dish.

5. People (*try, tries*) to keep doctors away with apples.

6. Beef producers (*advertise, advertises*) that beef is real food for real people.

7. In other ads, pork producers (*say, says*) that pork is the other white meat.

8. Gourmet cooks (*spend, spends*) hours preparing elegant dishes.

9. Time-conscious eaters (*heat, heats*) up frozen dinners.

10. Yogurt (*come, comes*) in one-serving containers or larger quantities.

11. Perhaps chocolate (*have, has*) more loyal fans than any other food.

12. Bagels (*taste, tastes*) wonderful with cream cheese, onion, tomato slices, and smoked fish.

13. Many adults (*find, finds*) a new day tough to face without a bracing cup of coffee.

14. Others (*start, starts*) the morning with healthful drinks like herb teas or fruit juices.

15. A serious athlete (*need, needs*) a high-protein diet.

Answers start on page 86.

Worksheet 18
Subject-Verb Agreement Problems

Directions: Carefully identify the subject of each sentence. Remember to check for compound subjects, inverted subject and verb, interrupters, and indefinite pronouns. Then underline the verb that correctly completes each sentence.

Text pages 96-105

1. Either Los Angeles or Boston (*win, wins*) the championship.

2. Nobody on the Minnesota Vikings (*complain, complains*) about a game in San Diego in January.

3. All of the Brewers' infielders (*was, were*) batting above .300 at the All-Star break.

4. Why (*do, does*) "The Star-Spangled Banner" open every baseball game?

5. Hot dogs and beer (*give, gives*) a Cubs game much of its flavor.

6. The sportscasters in the blimp (*focus, focuses*) their attention on the cheerleaders.

7. Here (*come, comes*) the goalie out of the penalty box.

8. Watching football games (*are, is*) a regular Sunday pastime for many Americans.

9. Fourth in the batting order (*are, is*) Mike Schmidt.

10. Michael Jordan, along with Larry Bird, (*dominate, dominates*) the headlines.

11. There (*go, goes*) the jockey's hopes for winning the Triple Crown.

12. Every competitor in the Special Olympics (*have, has*) a handicap of some kind.

13. Neither her coach nor the spectators (*know, knows*) where she learned that triple somersault.

14. Both Arnold Palmer and Jack Nicklaus (*have, has*) perfected the come-from-behind tournament victory.

15. Dean Smith, along with the other North Carolina coaches, (*practice, practices*) with the team two hours a day.

Answers start on page 86.

Worksheet 19
More Unfinished Sentences

Text pages
92- 105

Directions: Complete the following sentences, making sure that your subjects and verbs agree. Use your imagination and write interesting, detailed sentences.

1. In this day and age, knowledge ___*of computers is very useful.*___

2. Every day, I _____

3. In general, my relatives _____

4. Women's magazines _____

5. The present demands of _____

6. My current commitment _____

7. Today passion _____

8. Nowadays my parents _____

9. Modern customs _____

10. Now that I am an adult, _____

11. Now the cat _____

12 Every month, Hortense _____

Answers will vary.

Worksheet 20
Editing Review—Verbs

Directions: Check all the verbs carefully in the following paragraphs. You should correct all kinds of verb errors. Revise these paragraphs for correct use of

Text pages 71-105

☑ verb forms

☑ verb tenses

☑ subject-verb agreement

Paragraph 1

On summer evenings in days gone by, folks sitted on their front porches. Kids run and played up and down the block. Friends droped by. The latest bits of gossip were exchanged. But times have changed. There isn't any adults on the front porches. People relaxed in backyards and on private patios, away from the street. Or they stays inside. Either television or air-conditioning lure them in. And nobody drops by without an invitation anymore.

Paragraph 2

A new therapy offeres new hope for hard-to-treat types of cancer. Heat therapy, or hyperthermia, destroying tumors in many patients. It work better than radiation in many cases. Hyperthermia used advanced microwave and ultrasound technology. Only cancerous areas of the body is heated. For example, patients with skin cancer receives hyperthermia treatments in some experimental programs. A small microwave machine sit next to the patient's cancerous skin. The microwaves heat the skin for one hour. The temperature of the heated body tissues rises to about 109 degrees. Patients sometimes felt heat but not pain.

Answers start on page 86.

Worksheet 21
GED Practice with Verbs and Sentence Basics

Directions: In the following passage, you'll need to watch out for all the types of errors covered so far in this workbook. The passage is followed by questions asking you to correct the errors. Choose the best answer to each question.

(1) In spite of increased consciousness about weight and health, America's children getting fatter. (2) They're extra weight sometimes brings them ill health. (3) Obese children also experience social problems more frequently. (4) Ironically, diets doesn't help children lose weight. (5) Instead, diets triggered psychological and physical hungers and lead to overeating.

(6) What are good ways for parents to help obese children? (7) Here is some suggestions. (8) First, don't use food as a bribe, or reward for children's behavior. (9) Don't push youngsters into trying new foods, cleaning their plate's, or eating items in a particular order. (10) Ideally, a variety of nutritious foods are offered to children at regular meal and snack times. (11) Spend time with your child in physical activities, such as bicycling swimming, and playing ball. (12) Finally, chose your own foods wisely in order to set a good example.

1. Sentence 1: **In spite of increased consciousness about weight and health, America's children getting fatter.**

   What correction should be made to this sentence?

   (1) insert a comma after *weight*
   (2) change *America's* to *Americas'*
   (3) replace *children* with *child's*
   (4) change *getting* to *are getting*
   (5) no correction is necessary

2. Sentence 2: **They're extra weight sometimes brings them ill health.**

   What correction should be made to this sentence?

   (1) replace *They're* with *Their*
   (2) insert a comma after *weight*
   (3) change *brings* to *bring*
   (4) change *them* to *they*
   (5) no correction is necessary

3. Sentence 4: **Ironically, diets doesn't help children lose weight.**

   Which of the following is the best way to write the underlined portion of this sentence? If you think the original is the best way, choose option (1).

   (1 doesn't
   (2) does not
   (3) didn't
   (4) did not
   (5) don't

4. Sentence 5: **Instead, diets triggered psychological and physical hungers and lead to overeating.**

   What correction should be made to this sentence?

   (1) change *diets* to *diets'*
   (2) change *triggered* to *trigger*
   (3) insert a comma after *psychological*
   (4) change *hungers* to *hunger's*
   (5) change *lead* to *led*

5. Sentence 6: **What are good ways for parents to help obese children?**

   Which of the following is the best way to write the underlined portion of this sentence? If you think the original is the best way, choose option (1).

   (1) are
   (2) be
   (3) were
   (4) was
   (5) will be

6. Sentence 7: **Here is some suggestions.**

   Which of the following is the best way to write the underlined portion of this sentence? If you think the original is the best way, choose option (1).

   (1) is
   (2) will be
   (3) were
   (4) was
   (5) are

7. Sentence 8: **First, don't use food as a bribe, or reward for children's behavior.**

   What correction should be made to this sentence?

   (1) change *don't* to *doesn't*
   (2) insert a comma after *as*
   (3) remove the comma after *bribe*
   (4) change *children's* to *childrens'*
   (5) no correction is necessary

8. Sentence 9: **Don't push youngsters into trying new foods, cleaning their plate's, or eating items in a particular order.**

   What correction should be made to this sentence?

   (1) change *Don't* to *Didn't*
   (2) remove the comma after *foods*
   (3) change *plate's* to *plates*
   (4) insert a comma after *or*
   (5) insert a comma after *items*

9. Sentence 10: **Ideally, a variety of nutritious foods are offered to children at regular meal and snack times.**

   Which of the following is the best way to write the underlined portion of this sentence? If you think the original is the best way, choose option (1).

   (1) are offered
   (2) is offered
   (3) have offered
   (4) are offering
   (5) will be offering

10. Sentence 11: **Spend time with your child in physical activities, such as bicycling swimming, and playing ball.**

    What correction should be made to this sentence?

    (1) change *Spend* to *Spending*
    (2) change the spelling of *activities* to *activitys*
    (3) insert a comma after *bicycling*
    (4) insert a comma after *and*
    (5) no correction is necessary

11. Sentence 12: **Finally, chose your own foods wisely in order to set a good example.**

    Which of the following is the best way to write the underlined portion of this sentence? If you think the original is the best way, choose option (1).

    (1) chose
    (2) choosing
    (3) you will choose
    (4) have chosen
    (5) choose

Answers start on page 87.

COMBINING IDEAS IN SENTENCES

Worksheet 22
Practice with Compound Sentences

Text pages
128-31

A *compound sentence* contains two complete thoughts linked together with a conjunction and punctuation. The most common conjunctions are *and, but, or, for, nor, so,* and *yet.* When you use one of these conjunctions to join two complete thoughts, place a comma before it.

The first sentence below incorrectly places a comma in front of the word *and* because *and* is not being used to join two complete thoughts.

INCORRECT: The women will speak to the mayor, **and** the city
council about the day care center.
CORRECT: The women will speak to the mayor, **and** I will speak to
the city council.

Directions: In each of the following pairs of sentences, one is a compound sentence and one is not. Circle the letter of the compound sentence in each pair and add a comma to make the compound sentence correct.

1. **a.** Fred Astaire died in 1987 at the age of eighty-eight, but he will be remembered for years to come.
   b. Fred Astaire died in 1987 at the age of eighty-eight but will be remembered for years to come.

2. **a.** A Soviet line of cars known as Lada is now on the market in Canada and may soon be for sale in the United States.
   b. A Soviet line of cars known as Lada is now on the market in Canada and the cars may soon be for sale in the United States.

3. **a.** An American Airlines jet pilot changed course without clearance and he flew too close to three other planes as a result.
   b. An American Airlines jet pilot flew too close to three other planes after changing course without clearance.

4. **a.** Two area politicians say that the *Observer's* story about local corruption contained deliberate lies so they are suing the paper.
   b. Two area politicians say that the *Observer's* story about local corruption contained deliberate lies and are suing the paper.

5. **a.** The weather forecast is calling for a high near ninety with a 40 percent chance of thunderstorms.
   b. The high today will be near ninety and there is a 40 percent chance of thunderstorms.

6. **a.** You can buy a one-year membership at the Y for $100 or you can pay each time you go.
   b. You can buy a one-year membership at the Y for $100 or pay each time you go.

Answers start on page 87.

Worksheet 23
Choosing a Logical Conjunction

Text pages
128-31

The following connecting words (*conjunctions*) are often used to join two complete thoughts: *and, but, or, for, nor, so, yet.* Each of these conjunctions has a different meaning. When you combine two ideas in a sentence, it's very important to choose a conjunction that shows the correct relationship between the two ideas.

> INCORRECT: I love my brother, **so** I wouldn't live with him.
> CORRECT: I love my brother, **but** I wouldn't live with him.

Directions: Fill in the blank in each sentence with a conjunction that shows the relationship between the ideas in the sentence. Use the conjunctions *and, but, or, for, nor, so,* and *yet.* More than one answer is correct for some sentences.

1. Cats may catch and play with insects, _____*but*_____ they usually don't eat them.

2. Many people feel that pit bulls should not be kept as pets, _____ they are a very dangerous breed of dog.

3. The dog escaped at 3:00 A.M., _____ his owner found him right across the street in the pond an hour later.

4. Caring for a pet doesn't have to be a lot of work, _____ children can learn valuable lessons from the responsibility.

5. Pets cost money to feed, _____ their veterinary bills can be substantial.

6. People who want an unusual pet might keep a boa constrictor, _____ they might choose a ferret.

7. Unlike roommates, pets don't play loud music or have houseguests, _____ do they use your towels and toothpaste.

8. Psychologists say that most pets are good for people, _____ they provide companionship and unconditional affection.

9. Don't feed your pet table scraps, _____ it will constantly beg you for food.

10. Some pet foods provide more nutrition than others, _____ you should ask your vet what the best foods are.

Answers start on page 87.

Worksheet 24
Using Connectors

Text pages
133-36

Connectors are also used to form compound sentences. In the following compound sentence, the connector is in dark type. Notice the semicolon before it and the comma after.

This year I have been promoted at work; **furthermore,** I have been elected president of the PTA.

Different connectors have different meanings. Always choose a connector that shows the relationship between the ideas in a sentence.

Directions: Choose a connector from the following list to complete each of the sentences below. Fill in the connector *and* the necessary punctuation to complete each sentence. For most sentences, more than one answer is possible.

moreover	nevertheless	for instance
furthermore	therefore	for example
in addition	consequently	then
however	otherwise	

1. We hear frequent complaints about stress nowadays _____ many of us can't seem to reduce the stress in our lives.

2. Stress may actually be necessary _____ many of us would never get anything done without a little pressure!

3. Stress is not going to disappear from our lives _____ we need to learn to live with it.

4. Exercise is a good stress reliever _____ a brisk walk is relaxing and convenient for almost anyone.

5. Telling the truth in a stressful situation is a good strategy _____ tell your boss when a project isn't going well instead of hiding the problem.

6. Tell the people around you that you are under stress _____ they can be emotionally supportive.

7. Don't try to do too many things at once _____ keep in mind that every big job is accomplished one little thing at a time.

8. Many of us need to say "no" more often _____ we will end up trying to make everybody happy except ourselves.

Answers start on page 87.

Worksheet 25
Correcting Run-ons and Comma Splices

Two common mistakes with compound sentences are the run-on and the comma splice. A *run-on* jams two independent clauses together with no connecting words or punctuation. A *comma splice* puts two independent clauses together with a comma but no conjunction.

Text pages 137-39

RUN-ON: Jason claims he paid the **rent I** don't believe him.

COMMA SPLICE: Jason claims he paid the **rent, I** don't believe him.

CORRECT SENTENCE: Jason claims he paid the rent, **but I** don't believe him.

Part A

Directions: Each of the following sentences contains either a run-on or a comma splice. Correct each sentence, using a logical connecting word and correct punctuation or dividing the sentence into 2 sentences.

1. Air-conditioning is great on a hot summer night, not everyone can afford it.

2. Air conditioners are expensive to purchase and install, they also use a lot of costly electricity.

3. Window fans can work wonders they can create a cool breeze on the hottest night.

4. Two window fans can really cool things off have one fan blow into your apartment and another blow out.

5. Fans are not expensive to buy they also don't use a lot of electricity.

6. Measure your window before selecting a window fan otherwise you may buy a fan too large to fit on your windowsill.

Part B

Directions: Rewrite the following paragraph, correcting all the run-ons and comma splices.

Using over-the-counter drugs properly is very important, making mistakes with them can be dangerous. Most people want to just pop the pills they don't want to read the directions. Here's one case in which that attitude could backfire. Benedryl is a popular over-the-counter allergy medicine the warning on the package says that it causes drowsiness. An ingredient in Benedryl is also used in products like Sominex 3 that help people get to sleep at night. This allergy medicine could put you to sleep, don't take it and then get behind the wheel of a car!

Answers start on page 87.

Worksheet 26
Forming Complex Sentences

Text pages
139-45

Directions: Combine each of the following pairs of clauses into a complex sentence using the conjunction you are given. If you put the conjunction first in the sentence, remember to put a comma between the clauses. Write on a separate sheet of paper.

Example: although
   a. many viewers don't realize this
   b. the television show "The People's Court" is a real court

Although many viewers don't realize this, the television show "The People's Court" is a real court.

1. *because*
   a. the Friday night cop and detective shows are violent
   b. many parents don't allow their children to watch them

2. *when*
   a. viewers see lots of ads for beer, cars, and shaving cream
   b. sports come on television

3. *if*
   a. people are unable to read
   b. they can get a lot of information from television

4. *before*
   a. televisions were common
   b. many families gathered around the radio every night

5. *whenever*
   a. a new cartoon appears on Saturday mornings
   b. a toy company wants to promote a new toy

6. *though*
   a. constant TV ads are annoying to most people
   b. few turn off their sets

7. *wherever*
   a. viewers willing to pay for TV can get relief from commercials
   b. cable television is available

8. *unless*
   a. some parents don't let their children watch TV at all
   b. homework and chores are finished

Answers start on page 88.

Worksheet 27
Eliminating Dependent Clause Fragments

A good way to check for fragments is to read backward, sentence by sentence, making sure each group of words is a complete thought.

Text pages 145-46

Directions: Rewrite each of the following paragraphs, eliminating dependent clause fragments by joining them to the preceding or following sentences. Use a separate sheet of paper.

Paragraph 1

When you ride a motorcycle. You can't act like you're driving a car. You need more reaction time, and your bike is more sensitive to changes in road conditions. A smart cyclist rides the paths of car tires. Because more oil and grease gets dripped in the center of a lane. If you are in a motorcycle accident. A helmet could save your life. Leather clothing could save your skin from being peeled off by pavement. No one should drive a motorcycle. Until he or she has taken lessons from a safe-driving school.

Paragraph 2

The quality of hospital care certainly will decline. Unless more people can be convinced to become nurses. A nursing shortage has begun to hurt hospitals all over the country. When hospitals are shorthanded. Nurses have to care for more patients and often must work overtime as well. But low pay, as well as a heavy work load, makes nursing an unattractive profession. Although beginning nurses may earn more than $20,000. The most experienced nurses seldom earn more than $30,000.

Answers start on page 88.

Worksheet 28
Identifying Correct Sentence Combining

Text pages
127-52

Directions: Read each pair of short sentences carefully. Then circle the letter of the combined sentence that best restates the meaning of the two short sentences.

Example: Amelia Earhart disappeared in 1937. She was trying to fly around the world.

    a. While she was trying to fly around the world, Amelia Earhart disappeared in 1937.
    b. Amelia Earhart disappeared in 1937 after she flew around the world.

1. In 1928 Earhart was the first woman passenger to cross the Atlantic by air. She became an instant celebrity.

    a. Although in 1928 Earhart was the first woman passenger to cross the Atlantic by air, she became an instant celebrity.
    b. In 1928 Earhart was the first woman passenger to cross the Atlantic by air; consequently, she became an instant celebrity.

2. She flew solo across the Atlantic in 1932. Her fourteen-hour, fifty-six-minute trip was a speed record.

    a. When she flew solo across the Atlantic in 1932, her fourteen-hour, fifty-six-minute trip was a speed record.
    b. She flew solo across the Atlantic in 1932 in fourteen hours and fifty-six minutes.

3. Over the next five years, Earhart broke several more speed records. She was the first aviator to cover several long routes.

    a. Over the next five years, Earhart broke several more speed records and was the first aviator to cover several long routes.
    b. Over the next five years, Earhart broke several more records; therefore, she was the first aviator to cover several long routes.

4. In 1937 she announced her plan to fly 27,000 miles around the equator. No aviator had ever completed this difficult route.

    a. Though no aviator had ever completed this difficult route, in 1937 she announced her plan to fly 27,000 miles around the equator.
    b. In 1937 she announced her plan to fly 27,000 miles around the equator; otherwise, no aviator had ever completed this difficult route.

5. Amelia Earhart and her navigator disappeared toward the end of this journey. No trace of them was ever found.

    a. Amelia Earhart and her navigator disappeared toward the end of this journey, and no trace of them was ever found.
    b. Amelia Earhart and her navigator disappeared toward the end of this journey, nor was any trace of them ever found.

Answers start on page 88.

Worksheet 29
Completing Combined Sentences

Directions: Read each pair of short sentences carefully. Then combine the two sentences into one, using the part of the combined sentence you are given. Be sure your combined sentence fully restates the meaning of the original sentences and is punctuated correctly.

Text pages 127-52

Example: Human beings do not naturally belong in the water. Their physical makeup is designed for living on land.

water, for their

Human beings do not naturally belong in the water, for their physical makeup is designed for living on land.

1. Nonswimmers should not go into water past their shoulders. They should not use floats or life jackets to go into deeper water.

   Even if they have floats

2. River and ocean currents are serious dangers to swimmers. They tend to carry swimmers away from shore.

   because they tend

3. Never try to swim against a current. Swim diagonally with it and make your way gradually to shore.

   current; instead

4. Many people believe that dangerous stomach cramps come from swimming after eating. These cramps are neither common nor extreme.

   Although many people

5. Swimming across a lake is a popular test of strength. A safer test is swimming around the lake, close to shore.

   strength, but a

6. Only a trained lifesaver should try to rescue a drowning person. A drowning person is frightened, irrational, and dangerous.

   and dangerous; therefore, only

7. Slides and diving boards can be trouble areas in a pool. Swimmers should be especially cautious when using them.

   pool, so swimmers

Answers start on page 88.

Worksheet 30
Identifying Correct Sentence Rewriting

Text pages
127-52

Directions: Read each sentence carefully. Then choose the rewritten version that best restates the meaning of the original sentence.

1. More women are drinking today than ever; in fact, two-thirds of adult women and 80 percent of teenage girls use alcohol.

    a. More women are drinking today than ever, but two-thirds of adult women and 80 percent of teenage girls use alcohol.
    b. More women than ever are drinking today, and two-thirds of adult women and 80 percent of teenage girls use alcohol.

2. Because the alcohol industry sees women as a growing market, women's magazines are full of ads for alcoholic drinks.

    a. Women's magazines are full of ads for alcoholic drinks now that the alcohol industry sees women as a growing market.
    b. The alcohol industry sees women's magazines as a growing market, so they are full of ads for alcoholic drinks.

3. Alcohol has some special dangers for women, so they must be careful in using it.

    a. The special dangers of alcohol for women, and they must use it carefully.
    b. Women must use alcohol with care, for it has some special dangers for them.

4. When women are with heavy drinkers, they are more likely to be raped or abused in some way.

    a. Women are with heavy drinkers and are more likely to be raped or abused in some way.
    b. Women are more likely to be raped or abused in some way if they are with people who are drinking heavily.

5. If mothers drink during pregnancy, their babies may be affected by a range of problems.

    a. Babies may be affected by a range of problems if their mothers drink during pregnancy.
    b. They may be affected by a range of problems if they drink during pregnancy.

6. While the threat of alcoholism may be most frightening, long-term drinking increases the risk of breast and other cancers, as well as other diseases.

    a. Alcoholism may be the most frightening threat, but long-term drinking increases the risk of many diseases, including breast and other cancers.
    b. Long-term drinking increases the risk of breast and other cancers, as well as other diseases, where the threat of alcoholism is most frightening.

Answers start on page 88.

Worksheet 31
Rewriting Sentences

Directions: Read each sentence carefully. Then finish rewriting it, using the first few words you are given. Be sure your new sentence fully restates the meaning of the original sentence and is punctuated correctly.

Text pages
127-52

Example: Most of us think we just don't have time for everything, but a little organization might make a big difference.

Though most of us

Though most of us think we just don't have time for everything, a little organization might make a big difference.

1. Many people don't set priorities, so they end up wasting time on unimportant tasks.

   When people

2. Identify your true goals; then you will know what tasks are most important to you.

   You will know

3. Scheduling lets you make time for what you want to do; furthermore, you can relax when you know that you have a plan for the day.

   While a schedule lets you relax

4. Don't try to keep track of tasks in your head; instead, make a to-do list every morning and keep it handy all day.

   If you make a to-do list

5. If you tend to procrastinate on big projects, you may need to break them down into more manageable steps.

   You may need to break

6. Many of us like to do things ourselves, but learning to delegate tasks can save a lot of time.

   Although many of us

7. You don't have to do everything perfectly; instead, do necessary but unimportant tasks like housework in the fastest possible way.

   Do necessary but unimportant

8. You might find that you can have more time to yourself and a more balanced life if you get organized.

   Get organized

Answers start on page 88.

Worksheet 32
Special GED Questions

Text pages
127-52

Directions: This exercise will help you practice a special type of GED question that you'll find on the writing skills test. Choose the best answer to each question.

1. **You may never have heard of Sam Ross, but you've probably heard of his business.**

   If you rewrote this sentence beginning with

   Though you may never have heard of Sam Ross,

   the next word should be

   (1) but
   (2) you've
   (3) if
   (4) instead
   (5) probably

2. **Ross owns Fantastic Sam's, a chain of family hair salons. He himself is bald.**

   The most effective combination of these sentences would include which of the following groups of words?

   (1) salons; for example, he
   (2) When Sam owns
   (3) salons because
   (4) salons, yet he
   (5) salons for himself

3. **Ross is determined to open stores in any location with people and money; in fact, he has made a deal to open 2,000 franchises in Japan.**

   If you rewrote this sentence beginning with

   Because Ross is determined to open stores in any location with people and money,

   the next word should be

   (1) furthermore
   (2) in
   (3) deal
   (4) Japan
   (5) he

4. **Ross opened his first store in Memphis in 1974, and soon he had four stores in that area.**

   If you rewrote this sentence beginning with

   Once Ross had opened his first store in Memphis,

   the next word should be

   (1) soon
   (2) furthermore
   (3) then
   (4) and
   (5) after

5. **He started franchising in 1976. An employee wanted to open a store in Jackson, sixty miles away.**

   The most effective combination of these sentences would include which of the following groups of words?

   (1) in 1976, but an
   (2) in 1976 before an
   (3) If an employee wanted
   (4) in 1976 when an
   (5) in 1976 wanting to

6. **People pay Ross a one-time investment to open a Fantastic Sam's; then they never owe him another cent.**

   If you rewrote this sentence beginning with

   People never owe Ross another cent

   the next word should be

   (1) then
   (2) before
   (3) after
   (4) while
   (5) and

Answers start on page 89.

Worksheet 33
Sequence of Tenses

Directions: One of the verbs is left out of each of the following complex sentences. Fill in the correct tense of the verb you are given. Pay careful attention to showing the correct time relationship between the ideas in each sentence. In some cases, more than one answer may be correct.

Text pages 152-56

1. (*drive*) While that boy _____*was driving*_____, the driving teacher was sweating.

2. (*go*) Even though the car _____ sixty miles per hour, the eager dog jumped out the window.

3. (*support*) Deanna _____ her son until he is out of high school.

4. (*say*) Whenever Nicky answers the phone, she _____ something silly like "Ann Landers speaking."

5. (*make*) Though Sylvia _____ many mistakes before, none was as serious as this one.

6. (*escape*) While the girls _____ out their bedroom window, the boys were waiting around the corner.

7. (*burst*) While his math teacher was speaking, Duane _____ into uncontrollable laughter.

8. (*flirt*) Despite the fact that Mary Ann is dating Darell, she _____ with all the other boys.

9. (*finish*) After Phylicia _____ blow-drying her hair to perfection, she applied several layers of makeup.

10. (*get*) If Wendell _____ the lead in the play, he will have a swelled head for a year.

11. (*be*) After he had scored forty-two points in the championship game, Leonard _____ the talk of the town.

12. (*read*) While Rona _____ a bedtime story to her sister, the bathtub overflowed.

13. (*run*) As the circus was starting, the clowns _____ up and down the aisles.

14. (*leave*) Wherever that child goes, she _____ destruction behind her.

15. (*have*) If you ask Mrs. Shaw for some eggs, we _____ omelettes for dinner.

Answers start on page 89.

Worksheet 34
Editing Review—Sentence Combining

Text pages
127-58

Directions: Rewrite the following passage, correcting all the errors. You will find errors related to sentence combining—the problems you have been working on in Worksheets 22-33. Make sure that your sentences are

- ☑ combined with logical conjunctions or connectors
- ☑ punctuated correctly
- ☑ not comma splices or run-ons

Words, pictures, and mail now can be sent electronically packages still have to be delivered by hand. When you order something by phone a person has to bring it to your door. The post office has two busy package delivery services, Parcel Post and Express Mail, furthermore private delivery companies such as Federal Express and United Parcel Service are doing a brisk business. Why is the package delivery industry booming? Computers are making package delivery services faster and more reliable; so they are attracting and keeping more customers. Mail-order businesses may be growing because working men and women find catalog shopping more convenient.

As the demand for package delivery services grows, the demand for delivery truck drivers grows too. Drivers who work for UPS must be over twenty-one and have a good driving record. They don't need a college education, they have to be able to interact well with customers. The pay is good; for example the entry-level salary at UPS is about $10 per hour. If you are able-bodied, courteous, and a good driver. You might want to look into working for a delivery service.

Answers start on page 89.

Worksheet 35
Cumulative GED Practice

Directions: In the following passages, you will need to watch out for all the types of errors covered so far in this workbook. Each passage is followed by questions asking you to correct the errors. You'll also have to identify correct ways to combine and rewrite sentences. Choose the best answer to each question.

(1) Although the cold cereal industry started as a health food movement, many of today's cereals belong in the candy aisle. (2) What was the origin of cold cereal? (3) Granolas were first produced in the 1860s, the momentum for the industry began at the turn of the century. (4) A sanitarium director named John Harvey Kellogg figured out how to make flaked cereal, in fact he claimed that the process came to him in a dream. (5) He began to manufacture wheat flakes called Granose they were not a commercial success. (6) Kellogg made his big breakthrough, when he created cornflakes in 1902. (7) Other companies caught on to Kellogg's idea, and Post Grape Nuts, puffed rice, and shredded wheat, came on the market within a few years. (8) These worthy products continue to stand the test of time while hundreds of other cereals come and go. (9) Today's consumers are faced with a bewildering array of cereals and their nutritional claims. (10) A cereal might have eight, ten, or even thirteen "essential vitamins and minerals." (11) Some cereals contain about four teaspoons of sugar per serving; therefore, others have almost as much sodium as an ounce of baked ham. (12) Let the buyer beware, for no cereal can guarantee anyone a nutritionally sound diet.

1. Sentence 1: **Although the cold cereal industry started as a health food movement, many of today's cereals belong in the candy aisle.**

   Which of the following is the best way to write the underlined portion of this sentence? If you think the original is the best way, choose option (1).

   (1) movement, many
   (2) movement, but many
   (3) movement; however, many
   (4) movement many
   (5) movement. Many

2. Sentence 3: **Granolas were first produced in the 1860s, the momentum for the industry began at the turn of the century.**

   What correction should be made to this sentence?

   (1) change *Granolas* to *Granola's*
   (2) change *produced* to *producing*
   (3) insert *but* after *1860s,*
   (4) change *began* to *begun*
   (5) no correction is necessary

3. Sentence 4: **A sanitarium director named John Harvey Kellogg figured out how to make flaked cereal, in fact he claimed that the process came to him in a dream.**

   Which of the following is the best way to write the underlined portion of this sentence? If you think the original is the best way, choose option (1).

   (1) cereal, in fact he
   (2) cereal in fact, he
   (3) cereal, however he
   (4) cereal; in fact, he
   (5) cereal; however, he

4. Sentence 5: **He began to manufacture wheat flakes called Granose they were not a commercial success.**

   Which of the following is the best way to write the underlined portion of this sentence? If you think the original is the best way, choose option (1).

   (1) Granose they were
   (2) Granose, but they were
   (3) Granose, they were
   (4) Granose; but they were
   (5) Granose, but they was

5. Sentence 6: **Kellogg made his big breakthrough, when he created cornflakes in 1902.**

   Which of the following is the best way to write the underlined portion of this sentence? If you think the original is the best way, choose option (1).

   (1) breakthrough, when
   (2) breakthrough, then
   (3) breakthrough when
   (4) breakthrough and when
   (5) breakthrough,

6. Sentence 7: **Other companies caught on to Kellogg's idea, and Post Grape Nuts, puffed rice, and shredded wheat, came on the market within a few years.**

   What correction should be made to this sentence?

   (1) change the spelling of *companies* to *companyes*
   (2) change *Kellogg's* to *Kelloggs'*
   (3) remove the comma after *idea*
   (4) remove the comma after *wheat*
   (5) change *came* to *come*

7. Sentence 8: **These worthy products continue to stand the test of <u>time while hundreds</u> of other cereals come and go.**

   Which of the following is the best way to write the underlined portion of this sentence? If you think the original is the best way, choose option (1).

   (1) time while hundreds
   (2) time, so hundreds
   (3) time; furthermore, hundreds
   (4) time, hundreds
   (5) time but hundreds

8. Sentences 9 and 10: **Today's consumers are faced with a bewildering array of cereals and their nutritional claims. A cereal might have eight, ten, or even thirteen "essential vitamins and minerals."**

   The most effective combination of these sentences would include which of the following groups of words?

   (1) Although today's consumers
   (2) In spite of the fact that a cereal
   (3) claims, but a cereal
   (4) claims; nonetheless, a cereal
   (5) claims; for instance, a cereal

9. Sentence 11: **Some cereals contain about four teaspoons of sugar per serving; therefore, others have almost as much sodium as an ounce of baked ham.**

   What correction should be made to this sentence?

   (1) change *cereals* to *cereals'*
   (2) change *contain* to *contained*
   (3) replace *therefore* with *on the other hand*
   (4) change *have* to *are having*
   (5) no correction is necessary

10. Sentence 12: **Let the buyer beware, for no cereal can guarantee anyone a nutritionally sound diet.**

What correction should be made to this sentence?

(1) replace *Let* with *Let's*
(2) remove the comma after *beware*
(3) replace *for* with *yet*
(4) change *can* to *could*
(5) no correction is necessary

(1) As the female prison population grows, the unique plight of women inmates are coming to the surface. (2) When women are arrested, instead of asking for a lawyer. (3) They ask for they're children. (4) Most states have only one prison for women, and it's usually located in a rural area far from most inmates' families. (5) When a mother goes to prison, the effect on her children can be devastating. (6) Because women inmates are usually not discipline problems, they tended to be forgotten. (7) Their special needs are not met, they often do not get programs and services that are commonplace for male prisoners.

(8) Women usually are arrested for minor crimes such as, welfare fraud, prostitution, and shoplifting. (9) Often their husbands have forced them to commit these crimes to avoid physical abuse; furthermore, women in prison for a violent crime has often killed spouses who abused them over a period of years. (10) These women generally do not commit more violent crimes, so imprisoning them only further victimizes they and their children.

11. Sentence 1: **As the female prison population grows, the unique plight of women inmates are coming to the surface.**

Which of the following is the best way to write the underlined portion of this sentence? If you think the original is the best way, choose option (1).

(1) are coming
(2) came
(3) is coming
(4) had come
(5) will have come

12. Sentence 2: **When women are arrested, instead of asking for a lawyer.**

Which of the following is the best way to write the underlined portion of this sentence? If you think the original is the best way to write the sentence, choose option (1).

(1) instead of asking
(2) they ask
(3) they can't ask
(4) they don't ask
(5) instead they ask

13. Sentence 3: **They ask for they're children.**

Which of the following is the best way to write the underlined portion of this sentence? If you think the original is the best way, choose option (1).

(1) they're
(2) they be
(3) they were
(4) there
(5) their

14. Sentence 4: **Most states have only one prison for women, and it's usually located in a rural area far from most inmates' families.**

What correction should be made to this sentence?

(1) remove the comma after *women*
(2) replace *and* with *because*
(3) replace *it's* with *its*
(4) change *inmates'* to *inmate's*
(5) no correction is necessary

15. Sentence 5: **When a mother goes to prison, the effect on her children can be devastating.**

If you rewrote this sentence beginning with

For children, the results can be devastating

the next word should be

(1) when
(2) a
(3) that
(4) so
(5) goes

16. Sentence 6: **Because women inmates are usually not discipline problems, they tended to be forgotten.**

What correction should be made to this sentence?

(1) replace *Because* with *Whereas*
(2) insert a comma after *Because*
(3) remove the comma after *problems*
(4) change *tended* to *tend*
(5) no correction is necessary

17. Sentence 7: **Their special needs are not met, they often do not get programs and services that are commonplace for male prisoners.**

Which of the following is the best way to write the underlined portion of this sentence? If you think the original is the best way, choose option (1).

(1) Their special needs are not met, they
(2) Although their special needs are not met, they
(3) Their special needs are not met; consequently, they
(4) Their special needs are not met they
(5) Their special needs are not met, and they

18. Sentence 8: **Women usually are arrested for minor crimes such as, welfare fraud, prostitution, and shoplifting.**

What correction should be made to this sentence?

(1) change *are arrested* to *were arrested*
(2) change *crimes* to *crime's*
(3) remove the comma after *as*
(4) remove the comma after *fraud*
(5) no correction is necessary

19. Sentence 9: **Often their husbands have forced them to commit these crimes to avoid physical abuse; furthermore, women in prison for a violent crime has often killed spouses who abused them over a period of years.**

What correction should be made to this sentence?

(1) replace *their* with *they're*
(2) remove the comma after *furthermore*
(3) replace *furthermore* with *however*
(4) change *has* to *have*
(5) change *years* to *year's*

20. Sentence 10: **These women generally do not commit more violent crimes, so imprisoning them only further victimizes they and their children.**

What correction should be made to this sentence?

(1) change the spelling of *women* to *womans*
(2) change *do* to *does*
(3) replace *so* with *but*
(4) change *they* to *them*
(5) no correction is necessary

Answers start on page 89.

KEEPING YOUR STORY STRAIGHT

Worksheet 36
Placing Modifiers in Sentences

Text pages
182-87

A modifying phrase should always be placed as close as possible to the word it modifies. In the following example, the modifying phrase is *with wet diapers.* Notice how the meaning of the sentence changes depending on where the modifying phrase is placed.

> INCORRECT: The screaming baby was held by the mother **with wet diapers**.
>
> CORRECT: The screaming baby **with wet diapers** was held by the mother.

Note that if the modifying phrase comes first in a sentence, a comma should come after it.

> INCORRECT: **Crying with happiness** the man embraced his son.
>
> CORRECT: **Crying with happiness,** the man embraced his son.

Directions: With each of the following sentences, you are given a modifying phrase. Rewrite each sentence, incorporating the modifying phrase correctly.

Example: Posters were hung all over the walls of our rooms.
with Day-Glo green splotches

> Posters **with Day-Glo green splotches** were hung all over the walls of our rooms.

1. The shag carpeting was an inch longer than the grass outside. *in the family room*

2. You were very comfortable, so getting up fast to answer the phone was tough. *sitting in a beanbag chair*

3. Housewives put away their irons and ironing boards as polyester clothing appeared on the scene. *breathing a sigh of relief*

4. Suddenly blue jeans and T-shirts became the national uniform for everyone. *under thirty*

5. People in jeans would trip over their pants or snag them in bicycle chains. *with bell bottoms*

6. TV news producer Mary Richards was one of the first career women depicted on television. *played by Mary Tyler Moore*

7. Seven shipwrecked adventurers provided the setting for another popular TV show. *struggling to get off a desert island*

Answers start on page 89.

51

Worksheet 37
Correcting Misplaced Modifiers

Text pages
182-87

A misplaced modifier can usually be corrected by moving it as close as possible to the word it modifies. Sometimes, however, you may want to change a few words or turn a phrase into a clause to make the meaning crystal clear.

Directions: Some of the following sentences contain misplaced modifiers. Underline the misplaced modifier in each incorrect sentence; then rewrite the incorrect sentences on a separate sheet of paper.

Example: The salesman in the yellow chair <u>with brown hair</u> is Steve Hicks.

The salesman with brown hair in the yellow chair is Steve Hicks.

1. Gesturing wildly with his paintbrush, Nancy watched the artist.

2. Lynn ordered the file cabinet from Storrs with three drawers and a walnut top.

3. The cook stayed too long in the walk-in freezer wearing only a thin blouse.

4. The workers taking an early lunch break were out of danger when the structure trembled.

5. Willing to assist me, I had no trouble finding a sales clerk.

6. Sandy's car has a dent in the door and a bumper almost dragging on the ground.

7. Missing after the rash of robberies, I kept searching for the valuable documents.

8. Jonathan emptied the dishes from the dishwasher in his underwear.

9. The letter was written by the lawyer containing all the details of the divorce.

10. The treasure map scrawled on the back of the old man's will led his heirs to a pot buried in the woods.

Answers start on page 90.

Worksheet 38
Correcting Dangling Modifiers

A modifier **dangles** when it doesn't have a word to modify. In the following sentence, the modifying phrase *lost in the wilderness* is a dangling modifier.

Text pages 187-89

> Lost in the wilderness, the faint path was impossible to follow.

In this sentence, the reader can't tell who or what was lost in the wilderness. You could correct this sentence in at least two ways:

> Lost in the wilderness, Kira could not follow the faint path.
>
> or
>
> When Kira was lost in the wilderness, the faint path was impossible to follow.

Directions: Some of the following sentences contain a dangling modifier. Some are correct as written. Underline any dangling modifiers, then rewrite the incorrect sentences on a separate sheet of paper.

1. Looking for the bathroom, I opened a door onto the fire escape.

2. Shoes and shirt must be worn to be served.

3. Typing frantically until 3:00 A.M., Larry's paper was finally finished.

4. The VCR broke while watching *Gone with the Wind* for the twelfth time.

5. While walking to work, Geraldine saw a holdup in a Toys-R-Us.

6. All transaction slips should be filled out before coming to the teller's window.

7. Anxious to get home in time for "L.A. Law," the bus seemed to creep at a snail's pace.

8. Our house was robbed while on vacation.

9. With time to spare, Greg finished the test and checked his answers.

10. Dripping with sweat, gallons of Gatorade were consumed by the exhausted runners.

Answers start on page 90.

Worksheet 39
Using Renaming Phrases

Text pages
189-91

A special kind of modifying phrase, a ***renaming phrase***, renames a noun. A renaming phrase always comes directly after the noun it modifies. These phrases are always set off from the rest of the sentence by commas.

Directions: With each of the following sentences, you are given a renaming phrase. Rewrite the sentence, inserting the renaming phrase into the sentence. Be sure to punctuate correctly.

Example: Oliver North was a central figure in the Iran-contra affair.
  a Marine lieutenant colonel

> *Oliver North, a Marine lieutenant colonel, was a central figure in the Iran-contra affair.*

1. Abigail Van Buren often recommends that people seek counseling.
   a columnist known as "Dear Abby"

2. Habitat for Humanity builds and renovates housing for low-income families.
   a nonprofit Christian group

3. Every four years the Olympic Games take place in a different nation.
   international amateur sport competitions

4. The victims of the criminal plot had signed over their life savings to Mr. Uzzle.
   a soft-spoken, friendly man

5. The residents of the group home are transported to a workshop every day.
   severely retarded adults

6. Three recording artists are featured on the album.
   a collection of sixties pop tunes

7. Governor Martin met with legislators today to discuss the new bill.
   a plan to dispose of radioactive waste

8. The drought has destroyed corn and soybean crops here in Mecklenberg County.
   one of the worst on record

9. Joshua Mayberry eats toast at every meal.
   inventor of the microwave toaster

10. This group of children is learning origami.
    the ancient Asian art of folding paper

Answers start on page 90.

Worksheet 40
Identifying Parallel Structure

For a sentence to have parallel structure, any compound elements must be in the same form. Compound elements are joined by *and* or *or*, and they may be in a series of two or more.

Text pages 191-95

NONPARALLEL: **Washing** the breakfast dishes and **she walks** the dog are Lina's chores.

PARALLEL: **Washing** the breakfast dishes and **walking** the dog are Lina's chores.

Directions: Choose the sentence in each pair that is in parallel structure. Underline the parallel parts.

1. **a.** Top stories in today's news are the explosion of a bomb in Paris and when a plane was hijacked in Rome.
   b. Top stories in today's news are the explosion of a bomb in Paris and a plane hijacking in Rome.

2. **a.** Studies suggest that cutting back on red meat, using whole grains, and eating raw vegetables can reduce the risk of cancer.
   b. Studies suggest that cutting back on red meat, using whole grains, and raw vegetables can reduce the risk of cancer.

3. **a.** When the weather is very hot, you should drink lots of water, stay out of the sun, and avoiding hard exercise will help.
   b. When the weather is very hot, you should drink lots of water, stay out of the sun, and avoid hard exercise.

4. **a.** A planned agenda and having a good chairperson are key ingredients for a good meeting.
   b. A planned agenda and a good chairperson are key ingredients for a good meeting.

5. **a.** When you are writing, do you spend more time drafting your piece or on revising it?
   b. When you are writing, do you spend more time drafting your piece or revising it?

6. **a.** When test-driving a used car, listen for irregular sounds and you should be making sure the car steers in a straight line.
   b. When test-driving a used car, listen for irregular sounds and make sure the car steers in a straight line.

7. **a.** Janice Butler was hit by a car, spent two months in the hospital, and lost her job.
   b. Janice Butler was hit by a car, spent two months in the hospital, and she lost her job.

Answers start on page 90.

Worksheet 41
Correcting Vague and Confusing Pronouns

Text pages
195-99

Directions: Each of the following sentences or groups of sentences contains a vague or confusing pronoun. Replace the problem pronoun with clear information.

UNCLEAR: Melanie decided to study medicine because **they** really
help people.
CLEAR: Melanie decided to study medicine because **doctors** really
help people.

1. More and more of Siler City's residents are commuting to work in larger cities nearby. This makes the town seem more like a suburb.

2. Morrison discussed the upcoming union election with Kendall; then he wrote a memo to all employees.

3. Day after day they tell us about disasters and tragedies all over the world.

4. When children and parents discuss something together, they often do a lot more talking than listening.

5. Reporting on the PTA Food Fair, it said that the fair raised $2,000 for special programs.

6. Mr. Lockheart helped his son Reggie write a prayer for the funeral service, and he read it aloud at the service.

7. The new rule outlaws smoking throughout the building. This means that people will have to go outdoors to smoke.

8. With temperatures below zero and high winds, it makes going outdoors risky.

9. Ms. Monahan has been working with Kristin Holmes to complete her training program.

10. The elderly are making up an increasing percentage of the population. This creates more demand for resources and services for this age group.

Answers start on page 91.

Worksheet 42
Agreement in Number and Person

Part A

Text pages
201-05

Directions: Correct the errors in pronoun agreement in the following sentences. You'll need to check for agreement in number and agreement in person. Some sentences have more than one correct answer.

Example: Parents planning to accompany children on the field

                        their
          trip should turn in ~~your~~ money by Tuesday.

1. When the company needed to recruit more workers, they contacted the state job service office.

2. When a person is job hunting, your best strategy is to make personal contacts through people you know.

3. Both Rick Benson and Michael Jameson have turned in his forms.

4. Employees wishing to transfer to the new Zebulon plant should turn in your request forms by Thursday.

5. Either Zelda or Mona will have their interview at 10:00 tomorrow.

6. Every female worker of childbearing age must be told of special precautions they should take on the job.

Part B

Directions: Correct the errors in pronoun agreement in the following paragraph.

    Raising kids is a tough job, and most parents could use a little help along your way. To meet one's needs, dozens of family resource programs have emerged across the country. These programs offer its services to all kinds of families. For example, in upstate New York, a group called Family Survival has been working with their rural clients since 1971. And in a city neighborhood in Chicago, you can find support and resources at a center called Family Focus. A woman in San Antonio, Texas, founded a center to cut the 80 percent high-school dropout rate they saw among Hispanic children.

Answers start on page 91.

Worksheet 43
Editing Practice

Text pages
182-205

Directions: Check the following paragraph carefully for errors in all the areas you have been studying in Worksheets 36-42. Make sure that you use correct modifying phrases, parallel structure, and pronoun reference.

Though many people never graduate from college, he or she may learn a lot from life. The University of Hard Knocks recognizes success without college degrees. Two newspapermen, Jim Comstock and Bronson McClung accidentally started the university in the 1950s. Saying it was from the University of Hard Knocks, Bronson had no college degree, so Comstock made him a handsome diploma. Other people would see it on the wall and want them; eventually, this led to an organization. Alumni of UHK include U.S. senators Barry Goldwater and Jesse Helms, multimillionaire W. Clement Stone, and there is a Honduran businessman. The president of UHK is Ezra Wilson a retired furniture store owner. Wilson says that UHK supports college education. He hopes that someday everyone will have a college degree and having put the University of Hard Knocks out of business.

Answers start on page 91.

Worksheet 44
Cumulative GED Practice

Directions: In the following passage, you will need to watch out for all the types of errors covered so far in this workbook. The passage is followed by questions asking you to correct the errors. You also may have to identify correct ways to combine and rewrite sentences. Choose the best answer to each question.

(1) In the past thirty years, doctors have learned more about treating patients physical symptoms than they did in the previous three centuries. (2) However, some people think that doctors have lost much of their knack for caring for the whole person. (3) Patients list their biggest medical complaint as the doctor-patient relationship in surveys. (4) The most common reason patients give for leaving a doctor is the doctor's poor communication skills. (5) As a result, medical schools are teaching doctors to be better listeners. (6) At some schools, faculty members use closed-circuit television to evaluate the bedside manners of its students. (7) Students are coached in using posture, tone of voice, and with facial expressions to convey their interest in a patient. (8) This is good for both the doctor and the patient. (9) Stress from a bad medical experience can be psychologically damaging to you. (10) After a patient has a good experience with a doctor, recovery may seem faster.

1. Sentence 1: **In the past thirty years, doctors have learned more about treating patients physical symptoms than they did in the previous three centuries.**

   What correction should be made to this sentence?

   (1) change *have learned* to *had learned*
   (2) change *patients* to *patients'*
   (3) change *they* to *he or she*
   (4) change *did* to *done*
   (5) change the spelling of *centuries* to *centurys*

2. Sentence 2: **However, some people think that doctors have lost much of their knack for caring for the whole person.**

   Which of the following is the best way to write the underlined portion of this sentence? If you think the original is the best way, choose option (1).

   (1) their
   (2) they are
   (3) they're
   (4) his
   (5) one's

3. Sentence 3: **Patients list their biggest medical complaint as the doctor-patient relationship in surveys.**

   Which of the following is the best way to write this sentence? If you think the original is the best way, choose option (1).

   (1) Patients list their biggest medical complaint as the doctor-patient relationship in surveys.

   (2) In surveys, patients list their biggest medical complaint as the doctor-patient relationship.

   (3) In surveys, patients list your biggest medical complaint as the doctor-patient relationship.

   (4) Patients list one's biggest medical complaint as the doctor-patient relationship in surveys.

   (5) In surveys, patients list one's biggest medical complaint as the doctor-patient relationship.

4. Sentences 4 and 5: **The most common reason patients give for leaving a doctor is the doctor's poor communication skills. As a result, medical schools are teaching doctors to be better listeners.**

The most effective combination of these sentences would include which of the following groups of words?

(1) skills, but medical
(2) Since medical schools
(3) skills; consequently, medical
(4) To be better listeners is the most common reason
(5) Although the most common reason

5. Sentence 6: **At some schools, faculty members use closed-circuit television to evaluate the bedside manners of <u>its</u> students.**

Which of the following is the best way to write the underlined portion of this sentence? If you think the original is the best way, choose option (1).

(1) its
(2) it's
(3) they're
(4) his or her
(5) their

6. Sentence 7: **Students are coached in using posture, tone of voice, and <u>with facial expressions to convey their interest</u> in a patient.**

Which of the following is the best way to write the underlined portion of this sentence? If you think the original is the best way, choose option (1).

(1) with facial expressions to convey their interest
(2) facial expressions to convey their interest
(3) to convey their interest with facial expressions
(4) conveying their interest with facial expressions
(5) expressing their interest facially

7. Sentence 8: <u>**This is good for both the doctor and the patient.**</u>

Which of the following is the best way to write the underlined portion of this sentence? If you think the original is the best way, choose option (1).

(1) This is
(2) This was
(3) Communication being
(4) Communication is
(5) Communication was

8. Sentence 9: **Stress from a bad medical experience can be psychologically damaging to <u>you</u>.**

Which of the following is the best way to write the underlined portion of this sentence? If you think the original is the best way, choose option (1).

(1) you
(2) them
(3) your patients
(4) him or her
(5) patients

Answers start on page 91.

CAPITALIZATION AND SPELLING

Worksheet 45
Capitalization Overview

Always capitalize names of specific people and places. Words derived from the names of specific people and places are also capitalized. Especially watch out for specific titles, specific places, and specific dates when you are deciding what to capitalize. Don't capitalize a word unless you have a reason to.

Text pages 237-41

I called **Senator** Jenkins last week. I told the **senator** that residents of our town would oppose his bill.

Directions: The following sentences may contain one or two capitalization errors. Circle the word or words that contain the errors. Some sentences may be correct as written.

1. When Hector Matheson attended this High School, the football field was on the east side of the building.

2. On Saturday a parade will start at the corner of Washington and Lee in downtown Sarasota, florida.

3. Christmas eve is a time of great anticipation for both children and their Mothers and fathers.

4. In the United States, Japanese and german cars are very popular.

5. Tourists from America will find that the Dollar buys less in Europe than it did in the past.

6. A family reunion is a good chance to see the aunts, uncles, cousins, and more distant relatives that live far away.

7. Take the Antelope Freeway to Horizon Drive, then go North to Mellow Lake and turn right.

8. Learning a Foreign language such as spanish or French greatly enhances a person's education.

9. All State governments now have the right to set speed limits on rural interstates up to 65 mph.

10. International Motors corporation will be accepting applications tuesday through Friday at its main office.

Answers start on page 92.

Worksheet 46
Using Spelling Rules

Text pages
245 - 50

Directions: Each of the following sentences contains one misspelled word. Circle the misspelled word and write it correctly in the blank. All the errors in this exercise involve adding prefixes and suffixes or applying the *ie/ei* rule.

1. I was immediately (refered) to the manager, who checked my receipt.

   referred

2. During leisure time, many single adults experience lonliness; however, marriage does not guarantee a blissful love life.

   _____

3. Accompanied by another department cheif, he waved a handkerchief from the height of the carriage.

   _____

4. The conscientious neighbors settled the grievance in a peacable manner and buried their hatchet.

   _____

5. During a continuous seige, the army tries every conceivable method to seize the specified target.

   _____

6. The courageous officer decieved his staff and was scolded severely.

   _____

7. Neither niece was carrying eight beautiful flowers when she dissappeared.

   _____

8. Before this occurrence, the mischievious thief surely should have been committed to jail.

   _____

9. Although I was disappointed, I found the changeable arangement to be predictable.

   _____

10. The dissatisfied customer weighed the controled substance and was relieved.

    _____

Answers start on page 92.

Worksheet 47
Correct Spelling of Soundalike Words

Directions: Each of the following sentences contains one misspelled word. All the errors involve common soundalike words. Circle the misspelled word and write the correct spelling in the blank.

Text pages 251-54

1. As the heroine entered the church in (witch) the service would be held, she felt that it was truly holy.

    _____*which*_____

2. Because the inspection was so through, the pair of horses was disqualified.

    _____

3. Of coarse, I knew the effect would be small.

    _____

4. A lot of lose wires were found at the site.

    _____

5. I already told Jim that it's alright if he comes.

    _____

6. The plane is stationery at the moment, but soon it will carry military personnel to Antarctica.

    _____

7. Your not certain whether the later train will get you there in time?

    _____

8. All members of the city council new of the morale problem in the fire department.

    _____

9. A pear and a sweet roll will make a nice desert.

    _____

10. The dinner sat in the booth past the door, trying not to breathe the cigarette smoke.

    _____

11. The moral of the story was altogether unclear, but the principle told it anyway.

    _____

12. My advise to you is to learn that lesson thoroughly.

    _____

Answers start on page 92.

Worksheet 48
Practice with Commonly Misspelled Words

Text pages 268-71

Directions: Circle the misspelled word in each group and write it in the space provided. If all the words are correct, put a *C* in the space.

1. hot-air baloon
   the dictator died
   in his innocence
   I will persevere

   _____

2. striking similarity
   run-down tenemant
   cordless telephone
   a perfect recipe

   _____

3. this momentous occasion
   losing a roommate
   a marble statue
   a mocking laugh

   _____

4. labor of love
   knowledge of tax law
   eligible bachelor
   needing asistance

   _____

5. addressed the envolope
   between a rock and a hard place
   delicious meat loaf
   inevitable downfall

   _____

6. fourth out of fourteen
   have patience
   recognize the difference
   tough discipline

   _____

7. reading is fundamental
   influential politician
   improving education
   with a vengence

   _____

8. plenty of exercise
   coffee and conversation
   in the audiance
   wretched stomachache

   _____

9. vacuum the living room
   useful priviledge
   probably ready
   in hot pursuit

   _____

10. professional manner
    kept in suspense
    got no sympathey
    not particularly likely

    _____

11. before you apply
    already attempted
    maintenance worker
    fancy maneuver

    _____

12. excellent opportunity
    questionable integrety
    obedient dog
    period of historical significance

    _____

Answers start on page 92.

Worksheet 49
Editing Practice

Directions: The following paragraph contains errors in spelling and capitalization. Circle words containing capitalization errors. Remember to look for words that are not capitalized and should be, as well as words that are capitalized and should not be. Cross out misspelled words and write the correct spelling in the margin.

Text pages 237-58

Aunt Myrtle's absence from our saturday gathering was quite a suprise. My eighty-year-old Aunt had been a loyal member of the informul group for years. We could only gess at the emergency that had interrupted her sckedule. Later, with extreem embarrassment, aunt Myrtle told me her Story.

At two oh-clock Saturday Afternoon, Myrtle and her Husband, Hector, finished dinner at The Countryside Restraunt. Out of curyosity, Hector looked at the bulliten board on the way out. He saw an advertisment for a hot-tub busness on Setlow street. Hector reminded my aunt that he was determined to try a hot tub. He perswaded her to go although she was quite ancxious. So they headed North on a City bus.

Despite my interest in this facsinating tale, Aunt Myrtle refused to describe there experiment furthur. However, she did ernestly recommend that I try it.

Answers start on page 92.

★ GED PRACTICE ★

Worksheet 50
Cumulative GED Practice

Directions: In the following passage, you will need to watch out for all the types of errors covered in this workbook. The passage is followed by questions asking you to correct the errors. You may also have to identify ways to combine or rewrite sentences. Choose the best answer to each question.

(1) Experts say that by age twenty an American has recieved 80 percent of his or her lifetime exposure to skin-damaging sunlight. (2) Every year, half a million Americans develop skin carcinomas, a form of cancer that can be treated easily. (3) A more frightening type of skin cancer malignant melanoma, strikes about 23,000 Americans every year. (4) They are fatal to about 25 percent of its victims.

(5) In a study of 107 melanoma patients at Massachusetts Genral Hospital, Doctor Arthur J. Sober and some of his associates found that the patients were likely to remember a severe sunburn during their teen years. (6) And australian researchers found that great exposure to sunlight in childhood increased the risk of melanoma. (7) A professor at the Yale School of Medicine, doctor Sidney Hurwitz, says that skin cancer rates are climbing. (8) He blames our outdoor-oriented lifestyle, and he points out that even young children are overly exposed to the sun's harmful rays. (9) Experts say that infants under six months should be kept completely shaded or covered. (10) Older babies and children should be treated with a sunscreen having a protection factor of fifteen or higher.

1. Sentence 1: **Experts say that by age twenty an American has recieved 80 percent of his or her lifetime exposure to skin-damaging sunlight.**

What correction should be made to this sentence?

(1) change the spelling of *American* to *Americain*
(2) change the spelling of *recieved* to *received*
(3) change *his or her* to *their*
(4) change the spelling of *to* to *too*
(5) no correction is necessary

2. Sentence 2: **Every year, half a million Americans develop skin carcinomas, a form of cancer that can be treated easily.**

What correction should be made to this sentence?

(1) change the spelling of *million* to *milion*
(2) change *Americans* to *Americans'*
(3) remove the comma after *carcinomas*
(4) change the spelling of *easily* to *easly*
(5) no correction is necessary

3. Sentence 3: **A more frightening type of skin cancer malignant melanoma, strikes about 23,000 Americans every year.**

What correction should be made to this sentence?

(1) change the spelling of *frightening* to *frightning*
(2) insert a comma after *cancer*
(3) remove the comma after *melanoma*
(4) change *strikes* to *striking*
(5) no correction is necessary

4. Sentence 4: **They are fatal to about 25 percent of its victims.**

Which of the following is the best way to write the underlined portion of this sentence? If you think the original is the best way, choose option (1).

(1) They are
(2) They be
(3) This was
(4) It is
(5) This being

5. Sentence 5: **In a study of 107 melanoma patients at Massachusetts Genral Hospital, Doctor Arthur J. Sober and some of his associates found that the patients were likely to remember a severe sunburn during their teen years.**

What correction should be made to this sentence?

(1) change the spelling of *Genral* to *General*
(2) change the spelling of *Hospital* to *Hospittle*
(3) change *Doctor* to *doctor*
(4) change the spelling of *associates* to *assosiates*
(5) no correction is necessary

6. Sentence 6: **And australian researchers found that great exposure to sunlight in childhood increased the risk of melanoma.**

What correction should be made to this sentence?

(1) change *australian* to *Australian*
(2) change *researchers* to *Researchers*
(3) change *found* to *finded*
(4) change the spelling of *great* to *grate*
(5) no correction is necessary

7. Sentence 7: **A professor at the Yale School of Medicine, doctor Sidney Hurwitz, says that skin cancer rates are climbing.**

What correction should be made to this sentence?

(1) change *professor* to *Professor*
(2) change *School* to *school*
(3) remove the comma after *Medicine*
(4) change *doctor* to *Doctor*
(5) change the spelling of *says* to *saies*

8. Sentence 8: **He blames our outdoor-oriented lifestyle, and he points out that even young children are overly exposed to the sun's harmful rays.**

If you rewrote this sentence beginning with

Blaming our outdoor-oriented lifestyle,

the next word should be

(1) and
(2) however
(3) he
(4) pointing
(5) as

9. Sentences 9 and 10: **Experts say that infants under six months should be kept completely shaded or covered. Older babies and children should be treated with a sunscreen having a protection factor of fifteen or higher.**

The most effective combination of these sentences would include which of the following groups of words?

(1) Since older babies and children
(2) Treating infants under six months
(3) Despite the fact that infants under six months
(4) covered, or older babies
(5) covered; furthermore, older babies

Answers start on page 92.

PRACTICE TEST

Directions: The following items are based on paragraphs that contain numbered sentences. Some of the sentences may contain errors in sentence structure, usage, or mechanics. A few sentences, however, may be correct as written. Read the paragraph and then answer the items based on it. For each item, choose the answer that would result in the most effective writing of the sentence or sentences. The best answer must be consistent with the meaning and tone of the rest of the paragraph.

You should do this test in no more than 75 minutes. When you are finished, check your answers and fill in the evaluation chart on page 82.

(1) Many parents wonder however public schools can provide their children with a good education. (2) Its important not to forget that parents' actions also affect a child's achievement in school. (3) The best students in school often does a lot of their learning at home. (4) Talking with children helps them pick up ideas, words, and sentence formation. (5) The most basic way to teach your children at home is to read to them. (6) One can also turn all kinds of daily activities into learning experiences; for instance, have your children help you make grocery lists and compare products at the store. (7) Let your child know that making mistakes is part of learning, and let them see you making mistakes.

(8) By getting involved with your children's school, they will learn better. (9) Children are more comfortable at school, and feel safer when their parents know the teachers and principal. (10) If you keep informed about your child's classes and assignments, you would be better able to evaluate a child's complaints or a teacher's comments. (11) Your child's learning experience will be richer and with more success if you help.

1. Sentence 1: **Many parents <u>wonder however public</u> schools can provide their children with a good education.**

Which of the following is the best way to write the underlined portion of this sentence? If you think the original is the best way, choose option (1).

(1) wonder however public
(2) wonder; and, public
(3) wonder, however public
(4) wonder whether public
(5) wonder whether, public

2. Sentence 2: **Its important not to forget that parents' actions also affect a child's achievement in school.**

What correction should be made to this sentence?

(1) replace *Its* with *It's*
(2) change the spelling of *affect* to *effect*
(3) change *child's* to *childs'*
(4) change the spelling of *achievement* to *achievment*
(5) no correction is necessary

3. Sentence 3: **The best students in school often does a lot of their learning at home.**

What correction should be made to this sentence?

(1) insert a comma after *school*
(2) change *does* to *do*
(3) change the spelling of *a lot* to *alot*
(4) replace *their* with *there*
(5) insert a comma after *learning*

4. Sentences 4 and 5: **Talking with children helps them pick up ideas, words, and sentence formation. The most basic way to teach your children at home is to read to them.**

The most effective combination of these sentences would include which of the following groups of words?

(1) formation, or the most
(2) When picking up
(3) formation to teach
(4) Talking and reading
(5) While talking with children

5. Sentence 6: **One can also turn all kinds of daily activities into learning experiences; for instance, have your children help you make grocery lists and compare products at the store.**

What correction should be made to this sentence?

(1) replace *One* with *You*
(2) change the spelling of *experiences* to *experiances*
(3) replace *for instance* with *then*
(4) replace *you* with *one*
(5) insert a comma after *lists*

6. Sentence 7: **Let your child know that making mistakes is part of learning, and let them see you making mistakes.**

What correction should be made to this sentence?

(1) replace *your* with *you're*
(2) remove the comma after *learning*
(3) replace *and* with *yet*
(4) replace *them* with *him or her*
(5) no correction is necessary

7. Sentence 8: **By getting involved with your children's school, they will learn better.**

Which of the following is the best way to write the underlined portion of this sentence? If you think the original is the best way, choose option (1).

(1) they will learn better
(2) they will have learned better
(3) he or she will learn better
(4) you will help them learn better
(5) your children will learn better

8. Sentence 9: **Children are more comfortable at school, and feel safer when their parents know the teachers and principal.**

What correction should be made to this sentence?

(1) change *are* to *be*
(2) remove the comma after *school*
(3) replace *their* with *they're*
(4) change the spelling of *principal* to *principle*
(5) no correction is necessary

9. Sentence 10: **If you keep informed about your child's classes and assignments, you would be better able to evaluate a child's complaints or a teacher's comments.**

Which of the following is the best way to write the underlined portion of this sentence? If you think the original is the best way, choose option (1).

(1) assignments, you would
(2) assignments, one will
(3) assignments, you will
(4) assignments you would
(5) assignments, they will

10. Sentence 11: **Your child's learning experience will be richer and with more success if you help.**

Which of the following is the best way to write the underlined portion of this sentence? If you think the original is the best way, choose option (1).

(1) with more success
(2) having more success
(3) give them success
(4) more successful
(5) filled with success

(1) As smoking becomes more and more restricted in both public and private areas, smokers are feeling increasing pressure to quit. (2) A wide range of programs, publications, and professionals have appeared to serve a growing clientele of smokers which want to become ex-smokers. (3) Researchers studying how Americans quit smoking report that 95 percent go cold turkey, meaning you stop abruptly. (4) These quitters can get self-help books, pamphlets, videotapes, and, tape recordings from sources like the American Lung Association. (5) The 5 percent of smokers who need more support can choose from thousands of programs. (6) These include workshops at hospitals and other nonprofit agencies, as well as commercial programs. (7) Some people even became research subjects for studies of ways to quit smoking. (8) Specialists have found that if it uses a combination of behavior modification and nicotine chewing gum, quitters may have an easier withdrawal. (9) However, regardless of the method, less than 20 percent of quitters remaining nonsmokers for longer than a year. (10) Most people who finally quit for good have tried to quit sevral times.

11. Sentence 2: **A wide range of programs, publications, and professionals have appeared to serve a growing clientele of smokers which want to become ex-smokers.**

    What correction should be made to this sentence?

    (1) insert a comma after *professionals*
    (2) change the spelling of *professionals* to *proffessionals*
    (3) change the spelling of *appeared* to *apearred*
    (4) replace *which* with *who*
    (5) no correction is necessary

12. Sentence 3: **Researchers studying how Americans quit smoking report that 95 percent go cold turkey, meaning you stop abruptly.**

    What correction should be made to this sentence?

    (1) change *Researchers* to *Researcher's*
    (2) change *Americans* to *americans*
    (3) change *quit* to *quits*
    (4) replace *you* with *they*
    (5) change *stop* to *stopped*

13. Sentence 4: **These quitters can get self-help books, pamphlets, videotapes, and, tape recordings from sources like the American Lung Association.**

    What correction should be made to this sentence?

    (1) replace *These* with *Them*
    (2) change *can* to *could*
    (3) remove the comma after *books*
    (4) remove the comma after *and*
    (5) insert a comma after *recordings*

14. Sentences 5 and 6: **The 5 percent of smokers who need more support can choose from thousands of programs. These include workshops at hospitals and other nonprofit agencies, as well as commercial programs.**

    The most effective combination of these sentences would include which of the following groups of words?

    (1) smokers, including workshops
    (2) programs such as hospitals
    (3) thousands, including programs
    (4) programs, including workshops
    (5) Including the 5 percent

15. Sentence 7: **Some people even became research subjects for studies of ways to quit smoking.**

Which of the following is the best way to write the underlined portion of this sentence? If you think the original is the best way, choose option (1).

(1) became
(2) becoming
(3) becomeing
(4) becomes
(5) become

16. Sentence 8: **Specialists have found that if it uses a combination of behavior modification and nicotine chewing gum, quitters may have an easier withdrawal.**

Which of the following is the best way to write the underlined portion of this sentence? If you think the original is the best way, choose option (1).

(1) they uses
(2) they use
(3) it, using
(4) it used
(5) she uses

17. Sentence 9: **However, regardless of the method, less than 20 percent of quitters remaining nonsmokers for longer than a year.**

Which of the following is the best way to write the underlined portion of this sentence? If you think the original is the best way, choose option (1).

(1) quitters remaining
(2) quitters remain
(3) quitters' remaining
(4) quitters had remained
(5) quitter's remain

18. Sentence 10: **Most people who finally quit for good have tried to quit sevral times.**

What correction should be made to this sentence?

(1) change *quit* to *will quit*
(2) insert a comma after *good*
(3) change *have* to *has*
(4) change the spelling of *sevral* to *several*
(5) no correction is necessary

(1) Computers have arrived in the supermarkets, especially at the cash register. (2) Most people are familiar with checkout scanners and even computerized voices quoting the price of each item. (3) Now two Kroger stores near Atlanta, georgia, feature self-checkout lanes that allow customers to scan bar codes on their own purchases. (4) As a product slides over the scanner, its description and price is displayed on a video monitor. (5) Customers recieve a paper receipt, which they take to a cashier at the front of the store.

(6) But computers were not just for the checkout lanes. (7) Using another new system stores change the prices of items already on the shelves. (8) Normally stores place paper or plastic price tags on the edge of a shelf, the Telepanel system uses a receiver, a transmitter, a battery, and a display tag containing a memory chip. (9) With this system in place, radio waves from a central computer can change any price electronically. (10) Computers can be labor-saving devices for the store; therefore, they help get information to the consumer. (11) Some supermarket computers record and analyze a shopper's purchases every week others provide recipes, menus, and shopping lists for the uncertain cook.

19. Sentence 2: **Most people are familiar with checkout scanners and even computerized voices quoting the price of each item.**

    What correction should be made to this sentence?

    (1) change the spelling *familiar* to *familier*
    (2) insert a comma after *scanners*
    (3) change *voices* to *voice's*
    (4) change the spelling of *quoting* to *quoteing*
    (5) no correction is necessary

20. Sentence 3: **Now two Kroger stores near Atlanta, georgia, feature self-checkout lanes that allow customers to scan bar codes on their own purchases.**

    What correction should be made to this sentence?

    (1) change *Atlanta* to *atlanta*
    (2) change *georgia* to *Georgia*
    (3) change *feature* to *features*
    (4) replace *that* with *who*
    (5) change the spelling of *their* to *there*

21. Sentence 4: **As a product slides over the scanner, its description and price is displayed on a video monitor.**

    What correction should be made to this sentence?

    (1) replace *As* with *However*
    (2) change *slides* to *slid*
    (3) remove the comma after *scanner*
    (4) replace *its* with *it's*
    (5) change *is* to *are*

22. Sentence 5: **Customers recieve a paper receipt, which they take to a cashier at the front of the store.**

    What correction should be made to this sentence?

    (1) change the spelling of *recieve* to *receive*
    (2) replace *which* with *who*
    (3) change *take* to *took*
    (4) replace *they* with *he or she*
    (5) no correction is necessary

23. Sentence 6: **But computers <u>were</u> not just for the checkout lanes.**

    Which of the following is the best way to write the underlined portion of this sentence? If you think the original is the best way, choose option (1).

    (1) were
    (2) being
    (3) will be
    (4) is
    (5) are

24. Sentence 7: **Using another new system stores change the prices of items already on the shelves.**

What correction should be made to this sentence?

(1) change the spelling of *Using* to *Useing*
(2) insert a comma after *system*
(3) change *change* to *have changed*
(4) change the spelling of *already* to *all ready*
(5) change the spelling of *shelves* to *shelfs*

25. Sentence 8: **Normally stores place paper or plastic price tags on the edge of a shelf, the Telepanel system uses a receiver, a transmitter, a battery, and a display tag containing a memory chip.**

What correction should be made to this sentence?

(1) insert a comma after *paper*
(2) insert *but* after *shelf,*
(3) insert a comma after *uses*
(4) insert a comma after *containing*
(5) no correction is necessary

26. Sentence 9: **With this system in place, radio waves from a central computer can change any price electronically.**

If you rewrote this sentence beginning with

With this system in place, a store can use radio waves from a central computer

the next word should be

(1) change
(2) can
(3) to
(4) where
(5) the

27. Sentence 10: **Computers can be labor-saving devices for the store; therefore, they help get information to the consumer.**

Which of the following is the best way to write the underlined portion of this sentence? If you think the original is the best way to write the sentence, choose option (1).

(1) store; therefore, they
(2) store, therefore they
(3) store; however, it
(4) store; in addition, they
(5) store; however, he

28. Sentence 11: **Some supermarket computers record and analyze a shopper's purchases every week others provide recipes, menus, and shopping lists for the uncertain cook.**

Which of the following is the best way to write the underlined portion of this sentence? If you think the original is the best way, choose option (1).

(1) week others provide
(2) week; while others provide
(3) week, while others provide
(4) week, while others providing
(5) week, others providing

(1) One of the most widely accepted standards for measuring the existence of hunger in a Nation is the infant mortality rate. (2) The infant mortality rate measures the number of infants per thousand who die before their first birthday. (3) When the infant mortality rate in a country is greater than 50 deaths per thousand live births, hunger is widespread and persistent. (4) A country with an infant mortality rate below 50 may still contain pockets of hungry people but hunger is no longer an overwhelming problem. (5) In every country in the world before 1900, the infant mortality rate is more than 50. (6) In the twentieth century, many nations shown remarkable success in controlling hunger and hunger-related disease. (7) In fact, seventy-five countries have ended hunger as a critical nationwide issue, and forty-one of them have accomplished this feat since 1960. (8) As a result, more than half of the people on this planet live in a country in which hunger is not a pressing national issue. (9) There is no single right ways to bring about the end of widespread hunger in a society. (10) Some countries have used land reform programs, in others food subsidies, collective agriculture, or family farming. (11) For every country that points to one technique as the key to success, there is another country that did not use that technique at all.

29. Sentence 1: **One of the most widely accepted standards for measuring the existence of hunger in a Nation is the infant mortality rate.**

    What correction should be made to this sentence?

    (1) change the spelling of *accepted* to *excepted*
    (2) change *Nation* to *nation*
    (3) insert a comma after *Nation*
    (4) change *is* to *being*
    (5) no correction is necessary

30. Sentence 3: **When the infant mortality rate in a country is greater than 50 deaths per thousand live births, hunger is widespread and persistent.**

    If you rewrote this sentence beginning with

    Hunger is widespread and persistent in a country

    the next word should be

    (1) is
    (2) where
    (3) and
    (4) however
    (5) greater

31. Sentence 4: **A country with an infant mortality rate below 50 may still contain pockets of hungry people but hunger is no longer an overwhelming problem.**

    Which of the following is the best way to write the underlined portion of this sentence? If you think the original is the best way, choose option (1).

    (1) people but hunger
    (2) people however hunger
    (3) people finding hunger
    (4) people, hunger
    (5) people, but hunger

32. Sentence 5: **In every country in the world before 1900, the infant mortality rate is more than 50.**

    What correction should be made to this sentence?

    (1) change *world* to *World*
    (2) remove the comma after *1900*
    (3) insert a comma after *rate*
    (4) change *is* to *was*
    (5) no correction is necessary

33. Sentence 6: **In the twentieth century, many nations shown remarkable success in controlling hunger and hunger-related disease.**

    What correction should be made to this sentence?

    (1) remove the comma after *century*
    (2) change *nations* to *Nations*
    (3) insert *have* before *shown*
    (4) change the spelling of *controlling* to *controling*
    (5) no correction is necessary

34. Sentence 7: **In fact, seventy-five countries have ended hunger as a critical nationwide issue, and forty-one of them have accomplished this feat since 1960.**

    If you rewrote this sentence beginning with

    In fact, out of seventy-five countries that have ended hunger as a critical nationwide issue,

    the next word should be

    (1) before
    (2) forty-one
    (3) and
    (4) accomplishing
    (5) more

35. Sentence 8: **As a result, more than half of the people on this planet live in a country in which hunger is not a pressing national issue.**

    What correction should be made to this sentence?

    (1) remove the comma after *result*
    (2) change *planet* to *Planet*
    (3) change *live* to *living*
    (4) insert a comma after *hunger*
    (5) no correction is necessary

36. Sentence 9: **There is no single right ways to bring about the end of widespread hunger in a society.**

    Which of the following is the best way to write the underlined portion of this sentence? If you think the original is the best way, choose option (1).

    (1) is no single right ways
    (2) was no single right ways
    (3) is no single right way
    (4) are no single right way
    (5) isn't any single right ways

37. Sentence 10: **Some countries have used land reform programs, in others food subsidies, collective agriculture, or family farming.**

    Which of the following is the best way to write the underlined portion of this sentence? If you think the original is the best way, choose option (1).

    (1) in others food
    (2) in others, food
    (3) while others food
    (4) while giving others food
    (5) while others have used food

(1) In many areas of rural America, Firefighters don't get paid. (2) Many of them also purchase their own equiptment, such as beepers and flashing lights that clamp to the roof of a car. (3) These volunteer firefighters may spend as much as twenty hours a week answering calls, maintaining the trucks, and attending training sessions. (4) Furthermore, they risk injury or death while working to save the lives and property of other people. (5) Why does these firefighters choose to spend their time and money to put their own safety at risk? (6) They care about their communities, they want to be ready to help their neighbors in an emergency.

(7) Volunteer firefighters are trained to handle a wide variety of fire emergencies. (8) They know how to fight a house fire and they learn to handle flammable materials such as propane gas. (9) Hospitals and technical schools instruct us in responding to medical emergencies as well. (10) In fact, local firefighters are likely to answer a medical call faster than an ambulance coming from a hospital in another Town. (11) Fast response from volunteer firefighters can mean the difference between life and death.

38. Sentence 1: **In many areas of rural America, Firefighters don't get paid.**

What correction should be made to this sentence?

(1) change *America* to *america*
(2) remove the comma after *America*
(3) change *Firefighters* to *firefighters*
(4) change the spelling of *paid* to *payed*
(5) no correction is necessary

39. Sentence 2: **Many of them also purchase their own equiptment, such as beepers and flashing lights that clamp to the roof of a car.**

What correction should be made to this sentence?

(1) replace *their* with *there*
(2) change the spelling of *equiptment* to *equipment*
(3) insert a comma after *beepers*
(4) change the spelling of *lights* to *lites*
(5) no correction is necessary

40. Sentence 3: **These volunteer firefighters <u>may spend</u> as much as twenty hours a week answering calls, maintaining the trucks, and attending training sessions.**

Which of the following is the best way to write the underlined portion of this sentence? If you think the original is the best way, choose option (1).

(1) may spend
(2) will have spent
(3) spent
(4) spended
(5) will spend

41. Sentence 4: **Furthermore, they risk injury or death while working to save the lives and property of other people.**

If you rewrote this sentence beginning with

Furthermore, they risk injury or death as

the next word should be

(1) working
(2) while
(3) work
(4) if
(5) they

42. Sentence 5: **Why <u>does these</u> firefighters choose to spend their time and money to put their own safety at risk?**

Which of the following is the best way to write the underlined portion of this sentence? If you think the original is the best way, choose option (1).

(1) does these
(2) do these
(3) do them
(4) does they
(5) did these

43. Sentence 6: **They care about their communities, they want to be ready to help their neighbors in an emergency.**

What correction should be made to this sentence?

(1) change *care* to *cared*
(2) insert *and* after the comma
(3) change *want* to *wanting*
(4) change the spelling of *neighbors* to *nabors*
(5) change the spelling of *emergency* to *emergancy*

44. Sentence 8: **They know how to fight a house <u>fire and they learn</u> to handle flammable materials such as propane gas.**

Which of the following is the best way to write the underlined portion of this sentence? If you think the original is the best way, choose option (1).

(1) fire and they learn
(2) fire, and learn
(3) fire and learn
(4) fire, they learn
(5) fire and will learn

45. Sentence 9: **Hospitals and technical schools instruct us in responding to medical emergencies as well.**

What correction should be made to this sentence?

(1) change the spelling of *Hospitals* to *Hospitels*
(2) change the spelling of *technical* to *tecknical*
(3) insert a comma after *schools*
(4) replace *us* with *them*
(5) no correction is necessary

46. Sentence 10: **In fact, local firefighters are likely to answer a medical call faster than an ambulance coming from a hospital in another Town.**

What correction should be made to this sentence?

(1) remove the comma after *fact*
(2) change *are* to *be*
(3) change the spelling of *answer* to *ansuer*
(4) insert a comma after *call*
(5) change *Town* to *town*

(1) Though it can save you money, living with a roommate is not a bed of roses. (2) For example, a roommate, like brothers or sisters, were likely to borrow your clothes—without asking. (3) And roommates are notorious for not cleaning up after themselves. (4) They can ruin a lifetime friendship in a couple of days with a sinkful of dirty dishes. (5) Then there are the bills. (6) Who pays for the unidentifiable long-distance calls? (7) Whose fault was it when the toilet stops up and the plumber comes for an expensive visit? (8) Who pays for the window that gets broken during a New Year's eve party? (9) In the winter, either you or your roommate are going to have to sleep in that bedroom that never gets warm. (10) In the Summer, you'll get to fight over the air conditioning if you're lucky enough to have it. (11) In between, there are bound to be arguments over whether it's warm enough to have the windows open. (12) A good roommate, a considerate person with habits similar to yours is worth his or her weight in gold.

47. Sentence 1: **Though it can save you money, living with a roommate is not a bed of roses.**

    If you rewrote this sentence beginning with

    Living with a roommate can save you money,

    the next word should be

    (1) when
    (2) it
    (3) not
    (4) is
    (5) but

48. Sentence 2: **For example, a roommate, like brothers or sisters, were likely to borrow your clothes—without asking.**

    Which of the following is the best way to write the underlined portion of this sentence? If you think the original is the best way, choose option (1).

    (1) were
    (2) be
    (3) was
    (4) are
    (5) is

49. Sentences 3 and 4: **And roommates are notorious for not cleaning up after themselves. They can ruin a lifetime friendship in a couple of days with a sinkful of dirty dishes.**

    The most effective combination of these sentences would include which of the following groups of words?

    (1) And roommates, who are notorious
    (2) themselves, whose lifetime friendship
    (3) With a sinkful of dirty dishes, notorious
    (4) Notorious for ruining lifetime friendships,
    (5) By ruining a lifetime friendship

50. Sentence 7: **Whose fault was it when the toilet stops up and the plumber comes for an expensive visit?**

    Which of the following is the best way to write the underlined portion of this sentence? If you think the original is the best way, choose option (1).

    (1) was it when
    (2) is it when
    (3) was it while
    (4) were it when
    (5) was it because

51. Sentence 8: **Who pays for the window that gets broken during a New Year's eve party?**

What correction should be made to this sentence?

(1) change *pays* to *paid*
(2) replace *that* with *who*
(3) change *broken* to *broke*
(4) change *eve* to *Eve*
(5) no correction is necessary

52. Sentence 9: **In the winter, either you or your roommate are going to have to sleep in that bedroom that never gets warm.**

What correction should be made to this sentence?

(1) change *winter* to *Winter*
(2) change the spelling of *either* to *ethier*
(3) replace *your* with *you're*
(4) change *are* to *is*
(5) insert a comma after *sleep*

53. Sentence 10: **In the Summer, you'll get to fight over the air-conditioning if you're lucky enough to have it.**

What correction should be made to this sentence?

(1) change *Summer* to *summer*
(2) replace *if* with *however*
(3) replace *you're* with *your*
(4) change the spelling of *enough* to *enouph*
(5) no correction is necessary

54. Sentence 11: **In between, there are bound to be arguments over whether it's warm enough to have the windows open.**

What correction should be made to this sentence?

(1) remove the comma after *between*
(2) replace *there are* with *they're*
(3) change the spelling of *arguments* to *arguements*
(4) replace *it's* with *its*
(5) no correction is necessary

55. Sentence 12: **A good roommate, a considerate person with habits similar to yours is worth his or her weight in gold.**

What correction should be made to this sentence?

(1) remove the comma after *roommate*
(2) change the spelling of *similar* to *similer*
(3) insert a comma after *yours*
(4) replace *his or her* with *their*
(5) no correction is necessary

Answers start on page 80.

Practice Test Answer Key

1. **(4)** *However* does not make sense because it implies a contrast. *Whether*, which means *if*, is a logical conjunction in this sentence.

2. **(1)** Substitute *It is* in the sentence to see that the contraction *It's* is correct. *Its* is a possessive pronoun.

3. **(2)** The subject, *students*, is plural, so it needs the plural form *do*.

4. **(5)** The combined sentence would read, "While talking with children helps them pick up ideas, words, and sentence formation, the most basic way to teach your children at home is to read to them."

5. **(1)** The pronouns *you* and *your* are used throughout the passage.

6. **(4)** The pronoun *them* incorrectly refers to the singular noun *child*.

7. **(4)** In the original sentence, the introductory phrase *By getting involved with your children's school* is a dangling modifier. In the corrected sentence, the phrase modifies *you*.

8. **(2)** The second part of the sentence is not a complete thought, so no comma is needed.

9. **(3)** The verb *would* incorrectly shows past tense. This passage is in the present and future tenses.

10. **(4)** The prepositional phrase *with more success* must be parallel with *richer*. In the corrected sentence, *richer* and *more successful* are in parallel form.

11. **(4)** The relative pronoun *which* cannot refer to people.

12. **(4)** The pronoun must refer to Americans who quit smoking, so it must be *they*. The pronoun *you* is not used in the passage.

13. **(4)** No comma should come after *and*.

14. **(4)** The combined sentence would read, "The 5 percent of smokers who need more support can choose from thousands of programs, including workshops at hospitals and other nonprofit agencies, as well as commercial programs."

15. **(5)** Since the passage is written in the present tense, *became* must be changed to the present-tense form *become*.

16. **(2)** The pronoun *they* and the plural verb *use* correctly refer back to *Specialists*.

17. **(2)** The original sentence is a fragment because the verb form *remaining* needs a helping verb.

18. **(4)** This is a commonly misspelled word.

19. **(5)** This sentence is correct as written.

20. **(2)** The names of cities and states, such as *Atlanta* and *Georgia*, are always capitalized.

21. **(5)** The subject of this verb is *description and price*. Compound subjects joined by *and* are always plural.

22. **(1)** The rule is *i* before *e* except after *c*.

23. **(5)** The passage is written in the present tense.

24. **(2)** Set off an introductory phrase with a comma.

25. **(2)** The original sentence is a comma splice. Adding the conjunction *but* joins the two complete thoughts correctly.

26. **(3)** The rewritten sentence would read, "With this system in place, a store can use radio waves from a central computer to change any price electronically."

27. **(4)** The connector *therefore* is incorrect because it suggests a cause-and-effect relationship.

28. **(3)** The original sentence is a run-on. A conjunction is needed to separate the two clauses.

29. **(2)** General terms such as *nation* and *state* are never capitalized.

30. **(2)** The rewritten sentence would read, "Hunger is widespread and persistent in a country where the infant mortality rate is greater than 50 deaths per thousand live births."

31. **(5)** A comma is needed to separate the two complete thoughts.

32. **(4)** The words *before 1900* tell you to use the past tense.

33. **(3)** The verb form *shown* needs a helping verb.

34. **(2)** The rewritten sentence would read, "In fact, out of seventy-five countries that have ended hunger as a critical nationwide issue, forty-one have accomplished this feat since 1960."

35. **(5)** The sentence is correct as written.

36. (3) In the original sentence, the subject, *ways*, is plural. Choice (3) makes this subject singular—*way*—so that it agrees with the verb *is*.

37. (5) The second part of the sentence needs a verb and a conjunction to make sense.

38. (3) Since *firefighters* is not a specific title, it should not be capitalized.

39. (2) This is a commonly misspelled word.

40. (1) The sentence is correct as written.

41. (5) The rewritten sentence would read, "Furthermore, they risk injury or death as they work to save the lives and property of other people."

42. (2) The subject, *firefighters*, is plural, so it needs the plural verb form *do*.

43. (2) The original sentence is a comma splice, so it needs a conjunction to connect the complete thoughts correctly.

44. (3) Removing the second *they* gives the sentence a compound predicate.

45. (4) The pronouns *they* and *them* are used throughout the passage. *Us* and *we* are not used.

46. (5) The word *town* is a general term, so it should not be capitalized.

47. (5) The rewritten sentence would read, "Living with a roommate can save you money, but it is not a bed of roses."

48. (5) Since the subject, *roommate*, is singular, the present tense, singular verb *is* must be used.

49. (1) The combined sentence would read, "And roommates, who are notorious for not cleaning up after themselves, can ruin a lifetime friendship in a couple of days with a sinkful of dirty dishes."

50. (2) The other verbs in the sentence and in the passage are in the present tense.

51. (4) *New Year's Eve* is a specific holiday and should be capitalized.

52. (4) The subject is *you or your roommate*. When a compound subject is joined by *or*, the verb agrees with the part of the subject closer to the verb.

53. (1) The names of seasons are never capitalized.

54. (5) The sentence is correct as written.

55. (3) Renaming phrases must be set off by commas.

Practice Test Evaluation Chart

Use the chart below to determine the writing skills areas in which you need to do the most review. Circle any items that you got wrong, and pay particular attention to areas where you missed half or more of the questions. The column called "Satellite Review Pages" lists pages in Contemporary's *New GED Writing Skills Test,* and the column called "Exercise Book Review Pages" lists pages in this book. Go back to the appropriate pages when you need practice or review.

Skill Area	Item Number	Satellite Review Pages	Exercise Book Review Pages	Total Correct
Basic Sentence Structure	8, 13	30–43	11–13	_____/2
Nouns and Pronouns	2	44–57	14–17	_____/1
Verb Form and Tense	15, 17, 23, 32, 33, 40, 50	71–91	21–27	_____/7
Subject–Verb Agreement	3, 21, 36, 42, 48, 52	92–105	28–30	_____/6
Compound Sentences	25, 27, 31, 43, 44	128–39	34–37	_____/5
Complex Sentences	1, 28, 37	139–48	38–39	_____/3
Sentence Structure Problems	7, 9, 10, 24, 55	182–94	51–56	_____/5
Pronoun Agreement	5, 6, 11, 12, 16, 45	195–205	57	_____/6
Capitalization	20, 29, 38, 46, 51, 53	237–41	61	_____/6
Spelling	18, 22, 39	241–58	62–64	_____/3
Construction Shift	4, 14, 26, 30, 34, 41, 47, 49	150–52	40–44	_____/8
No Error	19, 35, 54			_____/3

Total Correct _____/55

ANSWER KEY

SENTENCE BASICS

Worksheet 1: Identifying and Rewriting Fragments
page 11

Part A

The rewritten sentences given below are only examples. There are many correct ways to rewrite the fragments as sentences.

1. **F** In many states, cars must stop for pedestrians in crosswalks.
2. **S**
3. **S**
4. **F** Never stop at the top of a freeway entrance ramp.
5. **S**
6. **S**
7. **F** Accidents result in higher insurance rates.
8. **F** Always use your turn signal when changing lanes.
9. **F** A learner's permit allows a person to drive with a licensed driver.
10. **S**

Part B

Here is one way to write the paragraph correctly. The four fragments are corrected and are in **boldface**.

More and more people are volunteering their time to help others. As many as 40 percent of adults report doing charitable work. **Some are involved in helping the elderly.** They might visit nursing homes, for example. **Or they might work in programs for youth like Big Brothers and Big Sisters.** Volunteers also work in Boys' Clubs, Girls' Clubs, and other community programs for children. **Churches often encourage people to volunteer by telling their members where their help is needed.**

Worksheet 2: Identifying the Simple Subject and Verb
page 12

1. pope — asked
2. (you) — Measure
3. candidates — are
4. values — Should be
5. farmers — sell
6. paintings — are
7. (you) — Tell
8. Members — voted
9. fools — do fall
10. records — are
11. supporters — were
12. receipts — totaled
13. (you) — Take
14. you — Have checked
15. inventor — lived

Worksheet 3: Compounding
page 13

1. Principals, superintendents, **and** administrators need leadership skills.
2. Homeless people sleep in the building at night **but** must leave by 6:00 A.M.
3. Sirens **and** barking dogs disturb the neighborhood.
4. The cause of the food poisoning could have been the meat, the potato salad, **or** the milk.
5. Brisk walking, swimming, **and** cycling are good aerobic exercise.
6. A recent poll showed that Americans are buying less beef **and** more chicken.
7. This state allows girls to marry at the age of fifteen **but** prevents boys from marrying before the age of seventeen.
8. Payton caught the forty-yard pass, ran the ball twenty-five yards, **and** scored a spectacular touchdown.
9. Wealthy parents can choose private schools **or** public schools for their children.
10. Tasteless humor **and** mechanical acting make this film poor entertainment.

Worksheet 4: Using Possessive and Plural Nouns
page 14

1. women
2. laws
3. family's
4. ex-wives
5. men
6. wives
7. penalties
8. children's
9. parent's
10. judges
11. states'
12. mothers'

Worksheet 5: Identifying Antecedents
page 15

1. Americans
2. Americans
3. Americans
4. shelters
5. woman
6. nephew
7. shelter
8. couple
9. couple
10. structure
11. structure
12. owners
13. shelters
14. man
15. shelter
16. shelter

Worksheet 6: Choosing Subject, Object, and Possessive Pronouns
page 16

1. any object pronoun
2. any subject pronoun
3. any possessive pronoun from column 1
4. I, you, he, she, we, they
5. me, you, him, her, us, them
6. I, you, he, she, we they
7. any possessive pronoun from column 1
8. I, you, he, she, we, they
9. mine, yours, his, hers, ours, theirs
10. me, you, him, her, us, them
11. me, you, him, her, us, them
12. mine, yours, his, hers, its, ours, theirs
13. I, you, he, she, we, they
14. my, your, his, her, our, their
15. any object pronoun

Worksheet 7: Pronoun Problems
page 17

1. I
2. It's
3. she
4. They're
5. Your
6. them
7. Who's
8. her
9. its
10. She
11. Its
12. Theirs
13. us
14. there's
15. Whose
16. They, we
17. me
18. You're
19. they
20. you're

Worksheet 8: Sentence Basics Editing Review
page 18

Here is a correct version of the paragraph. The corrections are in **boldface**. Some errors can be corrected in more than one way.

Programs for mildly retarded **teenagers teach** them basic life skills for more independent living. In one program, retarded teenagers come to school at a model apartment. At this school for living, the **teens** learn how to **cook and** clean. **They're** taught skills as simple as how to hold a broom. **They also learn more** complicated skills like cooking **breakfasts, lunches**, and dinners. **They** and **their** teachers also take trips outside the apartment. The students learn to order in **restaurants**, ride buses, and pay for movies and bowling. Parents report that the **students'** new skills are a big help at home. One mother says that **her** daughter now makes all the beds with hospital corners!

Worksheet 9: GED Practice in Sentence Basics
pages 19–20

1. (3)
2. (2)
3. (4)
4. (2)
5. (2)
6. (5)
7. (4)
8. (5)
9. (3)

USING VERBS

Worksheet 10: Simple and Continuing Tenses
page 21

1. read
2. is running
3. elected
4. will appear, will be appearing
5. is considering
6. was loading
7. will be pouring, will pour
8. will complete, will be completing
9. pays, is paying
10. will watch, will be watching

Worksheet 11: Using the Perfect Tenses
page 22

1. have formed
2. will have washed
3. had learned
4. will have entertained
5. had claimed
6. has guarded
7. will have boarded
8. had marketed
9. have reflected
10. has constructed
11. will have traveled
12. had accepted
13. had thrilled
14. have borrowed
15. will have selected

Worksheet 12: Review of Regular Verb Tenses
page 23

1. c
2. a
3. b
4. b
5. a
6. c
7. a
8. b

Worksheet 13: Unfinished Sentences
page 24

Answers will vary. Check your sentences with a friend or with your instructor.

Worksheet 14: Writing Irregular Verbs
page 25

1. a. wrote
   b. written
2. a. taken
   b. took
3. a. begun
   b. began
4. a. seen
   b. saw
5. a. drank
   b. drunk
6. a. froze
   b. frozen
7. a. rode
   b. ridden
8. a. wore
   b. worn

Worksheet 15: More Irregular Verbs
page 26

1. bitten
2. flew
3. taught
4. bought
5. swore
6. paid
7. stood
8. understood
9. slept
10. held
11. heard
12. found
13. meant
14. cost

Worksheet 16: Verb Tense in a Passage
page 27

Only the sentences that contained errors are reprinted below.

Passage 1
- They also **buy** more name brands.
- The average household discards more than 13,000 paper items each year and **tosses** out more than 1,800 plastic items.
- Plastics are hard to recycle, use up valuable petroleum, and **give** off toxic chemicals when burned.

Passage 2
- Nashville, the country music capital of the world, **panicked**.
- Today artists **are** looking back to Texas swing, 1950s honky-tonk and rockabilly, and bluegrass for inspiration.
- Their record sales **are** climbing.

Worksheet 17: Basic Subject-Verb Agreement
page 28

1. pick
2. is
3. contains
4. makes
5. try
6. advertise
7. say
8. spend
9. heat
10. comes
11. has
12. taste
13. find
14. start
15. needs

Worksheet 18: Subject–Verb Agreement Problems
page 29

1. wins
2. complains
3. were
4. does
5. give
6. focus
7. comes
8. is
9. is
10. dominates
11. go
12. has
13. know
14. have
15. practices

Worksheet 19: More Unfinished Sentences
page 30

Answers will vary. Check your sentences with a friend or with your instructor.

Worksheet 20: Editing Review—Verbs
page 31

Paragraph 1
On summer evenings in days gone by, folks **sat** on their front porches. Kids **ran** and played up and down the block. Friends **dropped** by. The latest bits of gossip were exchanged. But times have changed. There **aren't** any adults on the front porches. People **relax** in backyards and on private patios, away from the street. Or they **stay** inside. Either television or air-conditioning **lures** them in. And nobody drops by without an invitation anymore.

Paragraph 2
A new therapy **offers** new hope for hard-to-treat types of cancer. Heat therapy, or hyperthermia, **destroys** tumors in many patients. It **works** better than radiation in many cases. Hyperthermia **uses** advanced microwave and ultrasound technology. Only cancerous areas of the body **are** heated. For example, patients with skin cancer **receive** hyperthermia treatments in some experimental programs. A small microwave machine **sits** next to the patient's cancerous skin. The microwaves heat the skin for one hour. The temperature of the heated body tissues rises to about 109 degrees. Patients sometimes **feel** heat but not pain.

Worksheet 21: GED Practice with Verbs and Sentence Basics
pages 32-33

1. (4)
2. (1)
3. (5)
4. (2)
5. (1)
6. (5)
7. (3)
8. (3)
9. (1)
10. (3)
11. (5)

COMBINING IDEAS IN SENTENCES

Worksheet 22: Practice with Compound Sentences
page 34

1. **a.** Fred Astaire died in 1987 at the age of eighty-eight, but he will be remembered for years to come.

2. **b.** A Soviet line of cars known as Lada is now on the market in Canada, and the cars may soon be for sale in the United States.

3. **a.** An American Airlines jet pilot changed course without clearance, and he flew too close to three other planes as a result.

4. **a.** Two area politicians say that the *Observer's* story about local corruption contained deliberate lies, so they are suing the paper.

5. **b.** The high today will be near ninety, and there is a 40 percent chance of thunderstorms.

6. **a.** You can buy a one-year membership at the Y for $100, or you can pay each time you go.

Worksheet 23: Choosing a Logical Conjunction
page 35

1. but, yet
2. for
3. and, but
4. but, yet, and
5. and
6. or
7. nor
8. for
9. for, or
10. so

Worksheet 24: Using Connectors
page 36

Here are sample answers. More than one connector may be correct.

1. We hear frequent complaints about stress nowadays; **however,** many of us can't seem to reduce the stress in our lives.

2. Stress may actually be necessary; **furthermore,** many of us would never get anything done without a little pressure!

3. Stress is not going to disappear from our lives; **therefore,** we need to learn to live with it.

4. Exercise is a good stress reliever; **for example,** a brisk walk is relaxing and convenient for almost anyone.

5. Telling the truth in a stressful situation is a good strategy; **for instance,** tell your boss when a project isn't going well instead of hiding the problem.

6. Tell the people around you that you are under stress; **then** they can be emotionally supportive.

7. Don't try to do too many things at once; **moreover,** keep in mind that every big job is accomplished one little thing at a time.

8. Many of us need to say no more often; **otherwise,** we will end up trying to make everybody happy except ourselves.

Worksheet 25: Correcting Run-ons and Comma Splices
page 37

These are sample answers. There are several ways to correct run-ons and comma splices.

Part A

1. Air-conditioning is great on a hot summer night, **but** not everyone can afford it.

2. Air conditioners are expensive to purchase and install, **and** they also use a lot of costly electricity.

3. Window fans can work **wonders. They** can create a cool breeze on the hottest night.

4. Two window fans can really cool things **off. Have** one fan blow into your apartment and another blow out.

5. Fans are not expensive to buy, **and** they also don't use a lot of electricity.

6. Measure your window before selecting a window fan; **otherwise,** you may buy a fan too large to fit on your windowsill.

Part B

Using over-the-counter drugs properly is very **important, for** making mistakes with them can be dangerous. Most people want to just pop the **pills. They** don't want to read the directions. Here's one case in which that attitude could backfire. Benedryl is a popular over-the-counter allergy **medicine. The** warning on the package says that it causes drowsiness. An ingredient in Benedryl is also used in products like Sominex 3 that help people get to sleep at night. This allergy medicine could put you to **sleep, so** don't take it and then get behind the wheel of a car!

Worksheet 26: Forming Complex Sentences
page 38

For some sentences, more than one correct answer is possible.

1. **Because** the Friday night cop and detective shows are violent, many parents don't allow their children to watch them.
2. Viewers see lots of ads for beer, cars, and shaving cream **when** sports come on television.
3. **If** people are unable to read, they can get a lot of information from television.
4. **Before** televisions were common, many families gathered around the radio every night.
5. **Whenever** a toy company wants to promote a new toy, a new cartoon appears on Saturday mornings.
6. **Though** constant TV ads are annoying to most people, few turn off their sets.
7. Viewers willing to pay for TV can get relief from commercials **wherever** cable television is available.
8. Some parents don't let their children watch TV at all **unless** homework and chores are finished.

Worksheet 27: Eliminating Dependent Clause Fragments
page 39
Paragraph 1

When you ride a motorcycle, you can't act like you're driving a car. You need more reaction time, and your bike is more sensitive to changes in road conditions. **A smart cyclist rides the paths of car tires because more oil and grease gets dripped in the center of a lane. If you are in a motorcycle accident, a helmet could save your life.** Leather clothing could save your skin from being peeled off by pavement. **No one should drive a motorcycle until he or she has taken lessons from a safe-driving school.**

Paragraph 2

The quality of hospital care certainly will decline unless more people can be convinced to become nurses. A nursing shortage has begun to hurt hospitals all over the country. **When hospitals are shorthanded, nurses have to care for more patients and often must work overtime as well.** But low pay, as well as a heavy work load, makes nursing an unattractive profession. **Although beginning nurses may earn more than $20,000, the most experienced nurses seldom earn more than $30,000.**

Worksheet 28: Identifying Correct Sentence Combining
page 40

1. b
2. a
3. a
4. a
5. a

Worksheet 29: Completing Combined Sentences
page 41

1. **Even if they have floats** or life jackets, nonswimmers should not go into water past their shoulders.
2. River and ocean currents are serious dangers to swimmers **because they tend** to carry swimmers away from shore.
3. Never try to swim against a **current; instead**, swim diagonally with it and make your way gradually to shore.
4. **Although many people** believe that dangerous stomach cramps come from swimming after eating, these cramps are neither common nor extreme.
5. Swimming across a lake is a popular test of **strength, but** a safer test is swimming around the lake, close to shore.
6. A drowning person is frightened, irrational, **and dangerous; therefore, only** a trained lifesaver should try to rescue a drowning person.
7. Slides and diving boards can be trouble areas in a **pool, so swimmers** should be especially cautious when using them.

Worksheet 30: Identifying Correct Sentence Rewriting
page 42

1. b
2. a
3. b
4. b
5. a
6. a

Worksheet 31: Rewriting Sentences
page 43

Your sentences may not be exactly like these.

1. **When people** don't set priorities, they end up wasting time on unimportant tasks.
2. **You will know** what tasks are most important to you if you identify your true goals.
3. **While a schedule lets you relax** because you know that you have a plan for the day, it also lets you make time for what you want to do.

4. **If you make a to-do list** every morning and keep it handy all day, you won't have to keep track of tasks in your head.
5. **You may need to break** big projects down into more manageable steps if you tend to procrastinate.
6. **Although many of us** like to do things ourselves, learning to delegate tasks can save a lot of time.
7. **Do necessary but unimportant tasks** like housework in the fastest possible way; remember, you don't have to do everything perfectly.
8. **Get organized**, and you might find that you can have more time to yourself and a more balanced life.

Worksheet 32: Special GED Questions
page 44

1. (2)
2. (4)
3. (5)
4. (1)
5. (4)
6. (3)

Worksheet 33: Sequence of Tenses
page 45

Some of these sentences have two possible correct answers.

1. was driving, drove
2. was going
3. will support, is supporting
4. says
5. had made
6. escaped, were escaping
7. burst, was bursting
8. flirts, is flirting
9. had finished
10. gets
11. was
12. read, was reading
13. ran, were running
14. leaves
15. can have, will have

Worksheet 34: Editing Review—Sentence Combining
page 46

Answers can vary somewhat.

Words, pictures, and mail now can be sent **electronically, but packages** still have to be delivered by hand. When you order something by **phone, a** person has to bring it to your door. The post office has two busy package delivery services, Parcel Post and Express **Mail; furthermore, private** delivery companies such as Federal Express and United Parcel Service are doing a brisk business. Why is the package delivery industry booming? Computers are making package delivery services faster and more **reliable, so** they are attracting and keeping more customers. Mail-order businesses may be growing because working men and women find catalog shopping more convenient.

As the demand for package delivery services grows, the demand for delivery truck drivers grows too. Drivers who work for UPS must be over twenty-one and have a good driving record. They don't need a college education, **but** they have to be able to interact well with customers. The pay is good; for **example, the** entry-level salary at UPS is about $10 per hour. If you are able-bodied, courteous, and a good **driver, you** might want to look into working for a delivery service.

Worksheet 35: Cumulative GED Practice
pages 47–50

1. (1)
2. (3)
3. (4)
4. (2)
5. (3)
6. (4)
7. (1)
8. (5)
9. (3)
10. (5)
11. (3)
12. (4)
13. (5)
14. (5)
15. (1)
16. (4)
17. (5)
18. (3)
19. (4)
20. (4)

KEEPING YOUR STORY STRAIGHT

Worksheet 36: Placing Modifiers in Sentences
page 51

1. The shag carpeting **in the family room** was an inch longer than the grass outside.
2. You were very comfortable **sitting in a beanbag chair**, so getting up fast to answer the phone was tough.
3. **Breathing a sigh of relief**, housewives put away their irons and ironing boards as polyester clothing appeared on the scene.
4. Suddenly blue jeans and T-shirts became the national uniform for everyone **under thirty**.
5. People in jeans **with bell bottoms** would trip over their pants or snag them in bicycle chains.

6. **Played by Mary Tyler Moore**, TV news producer Mary Richards was one of the first career women depicted on television.
7. Seven shipwrecked adventurers **struggling to get off a desert island** provided the setting for another popular TV show.

Worksheet 37: Correcting Misplaced Modifiers
page 52

Some sentences can be corrected in more than one way.

1. Nancy watched the artist **gesturing wildly with his paintbrush.**
2. Lynn ordered the file cabinet **with three drawers and a walnut top** from Storrs.
3. **Wearing only a thin blouse**, the cook stayed too long in the walk-in freezer.
4. correct as written
5. I had no trouble finding a sales clerk **willing to assist me.**
6. correct as written
7. I kept searching for the valuable documents **missing after the rash of robberies.**
8. **In his underwear,** Jonathan emptied the dishes from the dishwasher.
9. The letter **containing all the details of the divorce** was written by the lawyer.
10. correct as written

Worksheet 38: Correcting Dangling Modifiers
page 53

These sentences can be corrected in several different ways.

1. correct as written
2. To be served, you must wear shoes and a shirt.
3. Typing frantically until 3:00 A.M., Larry finally finished his paper.
4. The VCR broke while we were watching *Gone with the Wind* for the twelfth time.
5. correct as written
6. Fill out all transaction slips before you come to the teller's window.
7. Because I was anxious to get home in time for "L.A. Law," the bus seemed to creep at a snail's pace.
8. Our house was robbed while we were on vacation.
9. correct as written
10. Dripping with sweat, the exhausted runners consumed gallons of Gatorade.

Worksheet 39: Using Renaming Phrases
page 54

1. Abigail Van Buren, **a columnist known as "Dear Abby,"** often recommends that people seek counseling.
2. Habitat for Humanity, **a nonprofit Christian group**, builds and renovates housing for low-income families.
3. Every four years the Olympic Games, **international amateur sport competitions**, take place in a different nation.
4. The victims of the criminal plot had signed over their life savings to Mr. Uzzle, **a soft-spoken, friendly man**.
5. The residents of the group home, **severely retarded adults**, are transported to a workshop every day.
6. Three recording artists are featured on the album, **a collection of sixties pop tunes**.
7. Governor Martin met with legislators today to discuss the new bill, **a plan to dispose of radioactive waste.**
8. The drought, **one of the worst on record**, has destroyed corn and soybean crops here in Mecklenberg county.
9. Joshua Mayberry, **inventor of the microwave toaster**, eats toast at every meal.
10. This group of children is learning origami, **the ancient Asian art of folding paper.**

Worksheet 40: Identifying Parallel Structure
page 55

1. b. Top stories in today's news are **the explosion** of a bomb in Paris and **a plane hijacking** in Rome.
2. a. Studies suggest that **cutting** back on red meat, **using** whole grains, and **eating** raw vegetables can reduce the risk of cancer.
3. b. When the weather is very hot, you should **drink** lots of water, **stay** out of the sun, and **avoid** hard exercise.
4. b. A **planned agenda** and a **good chairperson** are key ingredients for a good meeting.
5. b. When you are writing, do you spend more time **drafting** your piece or **revising** it?
6. b. When test-driving a used car, **listen** for irregular sounds and **make sure** the car steers in a straight line.
7. a. Janice Butler **was hit** by a car, **spent** two months in the hospital, and **lost** her job.

Worksheet 41: Correcting Vague and Confusing Pronouns
page 56

These sentences can be corrected in more than one way.

1. More and more of Siler City's residents are commuting to work in larger cities nearby. **This trend** makes the town seem more like a suburb.
2. Morrison discussed the upcoming union election with Kendall; then **Morrison** wrote a memo to all employees.
3. Day after day **reporters** tell us about disasters and tragedies all over the world.
4. When children and parents discuss something together, **parents** often do a lot more talking than listening.
5. Reporting on the PTA Food Fair, **the newsletter** said that the fair raised $2,000 for special programs.
6. Mr. Lockheart helped his son Reggie write a prayer for the funeral service, and **Reggie** read it aloud at the service.
7. The new rule outlaws smoking throughout the building. **Because of the rule**, people will have to go outdoors to smoke.
8. With temperatures below zero and high winds, **the weather** makes going outdoors risky.
9. Ms. Monahan has been working with Kristin Holmes to complete **Kristin's** training program.
10. The elderly are making up an increasing percentage of the population. This **increase** creates more demand for resources and services for this age group.

Worksheet 42: Agreement in Number and Person
page 57

Part A

Most of these sentences can be corrected in more than one way.

1. When the company needed to recruit more workers, **it** contacted the state job service office.
2. When **you are** job hunting, your best strategy is to make personal contacts through people you know.
3. Both Rick Benson and Michael Jameson have turned in **their** forms.
4. Employees wishing to transfer to the new Zebulon plant should turn in **their** request forms by Thursday.
5. Either Zelda or Mona will have **her** interview at 10:00 tomorrow.
6. Every female worker of childbearing age must be told of special precautions **she** should take on the job.

Part B

Raising kids is a tough job, and most parents could use a little help along **their** way. To meet **their** needs, dozens of family resource programs have emerged across the country. These programs offer **their** services to all kinds of families. For example, in upstate New York, a group called Family Survival has been working with **its** rural clients since 1971. And in a city neighborhood in Chicago, **families** can find support and resources at a center called Family Focus. A woman in San Antonio, Texas, founded a center to cut the 80 percent high-school dropout rate **she** saw among Hispanic children.

Worksheet 43: Editing Practice
page 58

Though many people never graduate from college, **they** may learn a lot from life. The University of Hard Knocks recognizes **the success of people without college degrees**. Two newspapermen, Jim Comstock and Bronson **McClung, accidentally** started the university in the 1950s. Bronson had no college degree, so Comstock made him a handsome **diploma, saying it was from the University of Hard Knocks**. Other people would see it on the wall and want **one;** eventually, **answering their requests** led to an organization. Alumni of UHK include U.S. senators Barry Goldwater and Jesse Helms, multimillionaire W. Clement Stone, **and a Honduran businessman**. The president of UHK is **Ezra Wilson,** a retired furniture store owner. Wilson says that UHK supports college education. He hopes that someday everyone will have a college **degree, and the University of Hard Knocks will be put out of business**.

Worksheet 44: Cumulative GED Practice
pages 59–60

1. (2)
2. (1)
3. (2)
4. (3)
5. (5)
6. (2)
7. (4)
8. (5)

CAPITALIZATION AND SPELLING

Worksheet 45: Capitalization Overview
page 61

The corrected words are listed below.

1. high school
2. Florida
3. Eve, mothers
4. German
5. dollar
6. correct as written
7. north
8. foreign, Spanish
9. state
10. Corporation, Tuesday

Worksheet 46: Using Spelling Rules
page 62

1. referred
2. loneliness
3. chief
4. peaceable
5. siege
6. deceived
7. disappeared
8. mischievous
9. arrangement
10. controlled

Worksheet 47: Correct Spelling of Soundalike Words
page 63

1. which
2. thorough
3. course
4. loose
5. all right
6. stationary
7. You're
8. knew
9. dessert
10. diner
11. principal
12. advice

Worksheet 48: Practice with Commonly Misspelled Words
page 64

1. balloon
2. tenement
3. correct as written
4. assistance
5. envelope
6. correct as written
7. vengeance
8. audience
9. privilege
10. sympathy
11. correct as written
12. integrity

Worksheet 49: Editing Practice
page 65

Aunt Myrtle's absence from our **Saturday** gathering was quite a **surprise**. My eighty-year-old **aunt** had been a loyal member of the **informal** group for years. We could only **guess** at the emergency that had interrupted her **schedule**. Later, with **extreme** embarrassment, **Aunt** Myrtle told me her **story**.

At two **o'clock** Saturday **afternoon**, Myrtle and her **husband**, Hector, finished dinner at The Countryside **Restaurant**. Out of **curiosity**, Hector looked at the **bulletin** board on the way out. He saw an **advertisement** for a hot-tub **business** on Setlow **Street**. Hector reminded my aunt that he was determined to try a hot tub. He **persuaded** her to go although she was quite anxious. So they headed **north** on a **city** bus.

Despite my interest in this **fascinating** tale, Aunt Myrtle refused to describe **their** experiment **further**. However, she did **earnestly** recommend that I try it.

Worksheet 50: Cumulative GED Practice
pages 66–67

1. (2)
2. (5)
3. (2)
4. (4)
5. (1)
6. (1)
7. (4)
8. (3)
9. (5)